BUSES
BY
DESIGN

GAVIN BOOTH

Ian Allan PUBLISHING

First published 2008

ISBN 978 0 7110 3326 9

© Gavin Booth 2008

Published by Ian Allan Publishing

an imprint of Ian Allan Publishing Ltd,
Hersham, Surrey KT12 4RG.

Printed by Ian Allan Printing Ltd,
Hersham, Surrey KT12 4RG.

Code: 0810/B3

Visit the Ian Allan Publishing website at
www.ianallanpublishing.com

The highly-standardised Leyland National introduced motorcar mass-production techniques to UK bus building and challenged
contemporary ideas about styling. This early example for Sunderland District was new in 1972.

Contents

For many observers a halfcab double-decker like this 1952 Leeds City Transport AEC Regent III with composite body by Charles H Roe represents the acme of traditional British coachbuilding skills, a teak-framed body designed to blend in with the exposed AEC radiator and featuring gently-curving and well-proportioned lines. After a period when bus body design seemed to lose its way, the importance of good styling is very much on the contemporary agenda.

Introduction

There are people who argue that it doesn't matter what buses look like – bus operators, bus bodybuilders, bus passengers. Buses are, after all, simply boxes providing a means of talking you from A to B and so they should be entirely functional; why on earth should they look attractive as well? In this book you will find examples of buses whose looks apparently owe something to this mind-set.

Fortunately, most operators and bodybuilders don't think like that and passengers have a right to enjoy the same attention to design and detail as car makers exercise.

Bus design is affected by so many factors – legislation, changing demand, passenger expectation, the economy, the development of new materials and technology – and this book looks at how these have affected the shape and look of buses over the past half-century or so.

More than a century ago, the first motorbuses were practical machines, their bodies owing much to the traditions and skills of coachbuilders who had cut their teeth on horse-drawn buses and trams, and early electric trams. As the motorbus industry grew so did confidence among builders and operators, and soon distinctive designs appeared. Major operators like London General and Midland Red had their own very individual and distinctive views on bus design, and their influence would continue – notably after London Transport had been formed in the 1930s, while Midland Red was a pioneer of several advanced features in the early post-World War 2 years.

Although this book concentrates on the post-1950 scene, what was happening then owed much to what had gone before, particularly when World War 2 forced bus manufacturers to put development work on hold – for the best part of a decade, as it would turn out.

The bus is an important part of the street scene throughout the UK and there are designs that have made such a significant contribution to the advances in styling. Views on design are, of course, subjective and it would be surprising if every reader agreed with every one of my views, but I hope readers will accept as a starting-point the importance of combining both function and appearance.

Today there is probably a greater recognition of the 'wow factor' in bus design than there has ever been, and we are seeing designers vying to produce buses that have the power to turn heads and attract passengers who may still see buses as cramped, dirty and smelly boxes, and no competition for their private cars.

And by buses I mean service buses, not luxury coaches. Anything, basically, designed to be used on what used to be called stage carriage services. So you may find a few dual-purpose vehicles that are essentially bus shells with more comfortable seats for use on longer-distance, interurban or even express duties, but to do the subject justice I have chosen to ignore vehicles with coach shells that were used on similar duties, or even those relatively few coach shells fitted from new with bus seats.

I have made extensive use of official photographs in this book. In the course of researching various books I have noted the wealth of such photos that resides in the Ian Allan archive. There is something fascinating about official photos, taken obviously to show the bodybuilders' products off to best effect – for the company records, for the customer and for publicity and advertising purposes. Inevitably these were taken by professional photographers using good-quality equipment – plate cameras in some cases – and bodybuilders had their favoured locations for these. Some posed buses outside the factory doors, while others used a quiet corner of the yard, or a nearby stretch of country road, perhaps in the local park or, curiously, in front of a local stately home. Few, sadly, waited to catch buses in service, but the great advantage of official photos is that they show buses exactly as they were on the day they left the factory, shiny and smelling of new paint and before operators made any adjustments to them. Without the grime of everyday service and the reflections and distractions of street scenes, they provide perfect portraits that will allow readers to understand and appreciate the design features mentioned in the text and captions.

The bus bodies covered in this book were built in the UK. For many years this was inevitable as operators had no need to turn elsewhere for their new buses. Indeed many operators looked to local businesses to supply their buses, and particularly in the case of municipally-owned fleets there were significant implications for local employment and the local economy. You only have to look at Alexander bodies for Scottish operators; the success of firms like East Lancs, Massey and Northern Counties in north-west England; Harkness and its successors in Belfast; Metro-Cammell bodies in Birmingham; Park Royal in London; Roe in Leeds. And on the chassis side, Albions in Glasgow, Daimlers in Birmingham and Coventry, Crossleys in Manchester, and Guys in Wolverhampton.

What was significant was that everything was built in the UK. Although a small number of imported chassis, mainly coaches, had found their way into UK fleets before World War 2, the importance of the bus industry to the postwar UK economy meant that there was little chance of any operator shopping elsewhere. That all changed in the 1960s when Metro-Cammell and Scania combined to challenge Leyland's dominant market position, and in the early 1970s Volvo started making inroads into the UK, followed by DAF and Scania, working on its own account. Most of the major European chassis builders followed over the next 30 years, but bus body building remained firmly in the UK.

Coach operators started to turn to the products of coachbuilders from continental Europe, particularly in the 1980s when they grew tired of the designs, or the durability, of bodies from the two main UK suppliers, Duple and Plaxton. Some of these builders produced small batches of bus bodies for UK operators, but it was the late 1990s before any significant inroads were made.

Vehicle dimensions and weights are initially expressed in the contemporary style, so the 1961 change in dimensions permitted 36ft x 8ft 2½in vehicles, while the 1967 change permitted 12m-long buses.

Vehicle dimensions and weight have played a crucial part in the way buses have looked and how they were built. From 30ft-long (9.1m) single-deckers in 1950 and double-deckers in 1956, buses grew to a maximum of 36ft (11m) from 1961 and 12m (39ft 4in) in 1967, and in line with EU standards from 2003 could be up to 13.5m (44ft 3in) on two axles, 15m (49ft 2in) on three axles and 18.75m (61ft 6in) for articulated vehicles; previously artics were limited to 18m (59ft 1in). Not every manufacturer or operator rushed for buses to the new maximum lengths, but some did. With the 2003 changes there has been less of a rush towards longer buses, though some single-deckers up to 12.6m long have been built, and a few operators have gone for three-axle buses for capacity.

Weight was an obsession in the late 1950s as passenger numbers dropped and fuel prices rose, and led to manufacturers developing some remarkably light and fuel-efficient buses. But weights crept up as dimensions increased and in recent years concern has been expressed by major operators about bus weights and the gauntlet has been thrown down to the manufacturers to produce lighter buses that are cheaper to run.

At the same time there are environmental concerns, which have been addressed in ever-stricter EU emissions legislation, but there is a strong lobby, led by London, for hybrid diesel-electric buses, which are currently under development by major manufacturers, but which will probably do little for vehicle weight in the early stages.

Various books on bus body builders have proved useful as references, published by Ian Allan publishing and Venture Publications, and various editions of Alan Millar's 'Bus & Coach Recognition' (Ian Allan) have proved invaluable.

Most of the photos in this book have come from the Ian Allan archive or from my own collection. There are also photos kindly supplied by Royston Morgan and Colin Hainstock from their collections. With fewer traditional official photos covering recent designs, Mark Lyons has supplied photos of some more recent types.

Gavin Booth
Edinburgh

Solid and functional
Bus design before 1950

Before we start we need to look back to consider the design of pre-1950 buses in some detail. Motorbus design evolved in the early years of the 20th century, but it took a handful of far-sighted visionaries to move things up a notch.

There is a clear sense of function when you look at iconic designs like London General's B type, built between 1910 and 1919. Here is a bus that today looks as anachronistic as pre-1920 motorcars do, but for a bus industry still finding its feet in an uncertain world there is no doubt that for all its rugged high-built looks, it is a well-balanced design. There are still echoes of the horsebus with the driving position outside the main body, exposed to the elements, and the high frame, and although closed-top tramcars had been around in the UK since the early part of the century the high centre of gravity of the B type didn't lend itself to the extra weight of a roof for the upper deck.

London was by far the main market for double-deck buses at that time and London designs were often all that was available for customers in the rest of the UK. The over-cautious Metropolitan Police prevented London's designs from developing organically and so top-covered double-deckers were only permitted in London from 1925, driving cabs with glass windscreens from 1927, and pneumatic tyres from 1929. The rest of the country, beyond the control of the Metropolitan Police, had adopted these improvements rather earlier.

London General nearly cracked it with the NS type in 1923, which incorporated the best features of its predecessors. It was low-built so

The first properly designed motorbus was the legendary London General B type, built between 1910 and 1919, but it is clear that the main passenger-carrying area still owed much to horse bus practice. The chassis is high-built, with deep steps leading to the interior and to the rear-mounted staircase. The upper deck passengers have no cover from the elements, but the driver at least has a canopy to shelter under. The B type was 19.1ft long with seats for 34 passengers, and weighed 4tons unladen. Although it looks crude by modern standards, the B type was a successful bus and paved the way for a long series of own-design buses for London service.

passengers could climb aboard more easily; it should have had a covered top and driver's windscreen from new but it would be four years before NSs took to the road in their intended form, and they had to wait another two years for permission to fit pneumatic tyres.

The London General NS type gradually gained the various refinements that were initially opposed by the Metropolitan Police. This later example dating from 1928 has a covered top and pneumatic tyres, but the driver is still out in the open. The low platform will be noted. The 52-seat NS was 26ft long and weighed 6.25tons unladen.

London had decided at an early stage that double-deckers were the answer to keeping the city moving and so its influence on single-deck design in the 1920s was rather less. It took manufacturers, notably Dennis, Leyland and Maudslay, to realise that low-built chassis were the answer and at a time when bodybuilding was often very much in the hands of firms situated close to bus operators, there were few designs that could be seen throughout the UK. One design that challenged this was the Leyland Lion PLSC model, low-built and designed to run on pneumatic tyres, which could be found in many fleets. While the Lion inspired a short-lived 'look' it would quickly appear dated when the even lower-built and sleeker designs of the late 1920s came along. These – most notably the AEC Regal and Leyland Tiger ranges – gave bodybuilders the confidence to develop sturdy and stylish designs that would set the pattern for the next 5-10 years. AEC and Leyland also made the running in double-deck design with their low-built Regent and Titan models.

The great majority of buses in the 1930s were front-engined and just as what was under the bonnet was changing dramatically as diesel engines became the norm and manufacturers like AEC and Daimler offered

preselective gearboxes to ease the driver's lot in urban traffic, the shape of buses was being transformed.

Covered-top double-deckers were *de rigueur* by the mid-1930s and the top deck was creeping forward over the driver's cab. Although some operators toyed with forward-mounted entrances, most notably London Transport, Midland Red and Trent, an open rear platform was by far the most common entrance layout; although Leyland's mould-breaking Titan TD1 was launched with an open rear staircase, the stairs quickly became enclosed in the overall box shape of the bus.

Single-deck buses were less clear-cut on entrance position. The forward entrance, just behind the front axle, was most common but there were significant operators who favoured rear entrances. This was a time when major groups developed their own recognisable styles, sometimes built for them by a range of bodybuilders.

But bus design has never stood still and in the 1930s chassis manufacturers were looking at pushing the envelope. AEC's side-engined Q, built in single-deck and double-deck form in the 1930s, gave a glimpse of what future generations of bus might look like. London Transport was the major customer for the Q and later worked with Leyland to produce two unusual types, the underfloor-engined TF Tiger and the rear-engined CR Cub. Interestingly, both designs retained the halfcab layout of their front-engined brothers, unlike the Q where bodybuilders eventually rose to the challenge of a full-fronted design.

The technical lessons learned from the Q, TF and CR types would resurface in the postwar years and it is fair to say that, had World War 2 not intervened and stopped normal development, underfloor- and rear-engined designs would have been with us some years before they actually became common.

The first motorbuses were timber-framed, just as horsebuses and contemporary electric trams were, and skilled craftsmen fashioned shapes from hard woods that gave buses subtle curves and meant that they were sturdy and safe. The exteriors were initially panelled in wood, but by the 1920s the use of sheet metal had become widespread, and this technique allowed for easy repair and replacement. In the late 1920s and early 1930s, at the same time as pioneering experiments with diesel engines and epicyclic gearboxes were taking place, bodybuilders were exploring metal-framed bodies and from the early 1930s manufacturers like Short Bros and Metro-Cammell were building metal-framed bodies in increasing quantities. Greater use had been made of aluminium alloy following World War 1, but normally only for body panelling; the use of aluminium for body framing would come later. For most bodybuilders the greater use of metal allowed them to streamline their processes as accurately-sized parts could be produced for easier assembly. Metal-framed bodies, it was argued, could be lighter, stronger and more durable, and safer in the case of accidents or fires.

Some builders and operators preferred to stick to timber-framed bodies, and this would be the situation during and in the years following World War 2, and timber-framed bodies clad in metal panels, and often with considerable metal reinforcement of the timber framing, became known as composite bodies. The term 'all-metal' was used for many of the early bodies that were strictly metal-framed, usually in steel, with aluminium panelling and with some wood content, typically for floors, for inserts in pillar sections and for interior finishing.

Among the British bodybuilders that started offering metal-framed bodies in the 1930s were Alexander, Brush, Cowieson, Crossley, English Electric, Leyland, Northern Counties, Park Royal, Roe and Short Bros. Some continued to offer composite or metal bodies, while Roe customers tended to prefer its famously well-built teak-framed composite bodies for some years to come.

Some builders got metal-framed bodies right first time, while others, notably Leyland, experienced problems with early examples. During World War 2 the basic Ministry of Supply specification for utility bodies called for composite construction, but Northern Counties was allowed to produce steel-framed bodies that often lasted longer than contemporary bodies built using poor-quality unseasoned timber.

In the 1930s there were attempts by operators and bodybuilders to create a more modern look, with full-fronted buses and buses that broke away from the essentially box-like shape of the bus with attempts at streamlining, which was very much in vogue at the time. Manchester Corporation's streamline design is probably the best remembered – and arguably most successful – of these.

But for many, full fronts and streamlining belonged on luxury coaches, and while double-deck buses were essentially functional machines there was no reason why they should not look well-proportioned and handsome.

London Transport – again – led the way with classics like its ultimate 1935 STL design and Leyland's 1938 body on its Titan TD5 chassis is another timeless style. The Leyland body style fitted to the TD5 and TD7 reappeared after the war fitted to the new Titan PD1 and PD2 chassis and provides a link between the 1930s and the 1950s.

Another design that stood the test of time was the London Transport single-deck 5Q5 type, built by Park Royal on AEC Q chassis in 1936. Unlike the bodies on LT's other Qs, the 80 5Q5s had entrances ahead of the front axle, a layout that would become very familiar on single-deckers some 15 years later.

Below left: The Leyland Lion PLSC Lion represented an advance for many operators with its low build and distinctive body style. This Leyland-bodied PLSC1 example was new to Ribble in 1926 and shows the two shallow steps to the saloon and the fully-enclosed body.

Below: The Leyland Titan TD1 really established the proportions of double-deckers for the next 30-40 years, with its low build and clean lines. The 'piano-front' profile over the driver's cab was a recognition feature – previously the upper deck on most double-deckers stopped behind the front axle. This Crosville 1930 example, seen in wartime guise, lasted in service until 1953.

Right: The side-engined AEC Q was an attempt to get away from the inevitable front-engined layout of buses and coaches. The Q enjoyed limited success in the mid-1930s, and London Transport proved to be its main customer. Most were single-deckers but there were five double-deckers; this was the first, built in 1934 with a Metro-Cammell metal-framed 56-seat body. The lines are clean and the bus looks surprisingly modern, apart from the short tail and the doorless entrance ahead of the front axle. The destination screen above the entrance seems rather superfluous.

Below: Most of London Transport's 233 single-deck side-engined AEC Qs had entrances behind the front axle for Country Area and Green Line work, but in 1936 LT bought 80 Central Area buses with Park Royal 37-seat setback front axles and doorless entrances. The neat body design provided a foretaste of new types more than a decade later, after World War 2.

And London Transport was also responsible for a design classic that would influence the look of new buses for the next 20 years, the RT type built on AEC Regent chassis and introducing a look that others would strive to copy – a low-built radiator with deep driver's windscreen, lines that flowed and the whole bus looking as if it had been designed from the ground up – as indeed it had been at London Transport's legendary Chiswick Works – rather than assembled using what was in the body parts bin. The first RTs had been built in 1939 and when production was forced to finish at the end of 1941, 151 had been built.

It may seem surprising, but even during the war when manufacturers were required to build to strict utility specifications some builders managed to produce buses that were surprisingly well-proportioned even if their specification was a far cry from the sleek and well-finished buses that appeared in the immediate prewar years. Northern Counties and Park Royal bodies were particularly handsome in a rugged way and when restrictions were eased these firms would continue to build bodies to what were essentially relaxed versions of the same designs.

And that was how it was for most suppliers in the immediate postwar years. With operators hungry for new bodies and the government urging manufacturers to export their products to help the war-damaged economy it was hardly surprising that many bodybuilders kept the pot boiling with updated versions of wartime and even prewar body styles. But in the background the major chassis builders were busily working on innovative designs that would radically affect the look of British buses forever.

Another innovative design for London Transport was the Leyland Tiger FEC, London's TF type. This had an underfloor engine and integrally-mounted 34-seat LPTB body built at Chiswick. The 27ft 6in long bus retained a separate driver's cab unlike postwar underfloor-engined buses that had a setback front axle and an entrance ahead of this. The body has a definite London look, both in the style of windows and the close attention to detail. It weighed 6.55tons.

Left: World War 2 buses were required to be functional, no-frills vehicles, but they could still be attractive – like this 1944 Maidstone & District Guy Arab with Park Royal bodywork. The basic body structure would serve Park Royal into the postwar period, complete with more relaxed finish and fittings. This bus, like many wartime chassis, would be rebodied in the postwar period.

Left: Several operators and manufacturers were keen to introduce the 1930s streamlined look on their vehicles, and while streamlining was most often applied to luxury coaches, some buses got the treatment too. This is a 1935 Leeds City Transport AEC Regent with metal-framed Weymann body. The bus has a full-width front, built around the AEC radiator, and while half of the side windows have flat bottom edges, the others are subtly curved, the effect being rather exaggerated by the livery style.

Above: A foretaste of things to come was provided by this 1943 rebuild of one of Midland Red's 1938 BMMO forward entrance FEDD types with a full-width enclosed radiator and mudwings. The standard FEDD body has been tweaked around the upper deck front windows, but it is the 'new look' front that would become a significant feature of postwar deliveries, with Midland Red leading the field.

Right: A more straightforward body style from the immediate prewar period that would go on to be built to broadly similar proportions until 1954 was the Leyland metal-framed style on Leyland Titan chassis. This is a 1940 Titan TD7 for Stockport Corporation; the very satisfying body shape is regarded as an all-time classic. This bus weighed 6.95tons.

The bus bears the number 3024 and text reading:

THE BIRMINGHAM & MIDLAND MOTOR OMNIBUS Co.Ltd.
BEARWOOD Rd. BIRMINGHAM.
O M SINCLAIR M.I.A.E. M.Inst.T.
GENERAL MANAGER.

MIDLAN

Left: Midland Red's prewar and wartime experimental work with rear-engined and underfloor-engined chassis allowed it to pioneer production of advanced designs in the early postwar years. This was a BMMO S6 with Brush 40-seat body, delivered in 1946, and built to 27ft 6in length, and this would be the general shape of single-deckers for some years.

Below: In spite of its pioneering prewar work on rear- and underfloor-engined single-deckers, London Transport resumed its renewal programme after the war with more conventional buses. This 1948 AEC Regal III with competent Mann Egerton body was typical of the last generation of full-size front-engined single-deckers. It was a 31-seater weighing 6.55tons.

Left: Metal Sections produced skeleton framing for other builders to complete. This is a frame on Leyland Titan PD2 chassis for Liverpool Corporation, that was finished by Duple (Midland).

Below: Bus chassis were delivered to bodybuilders like this, a bare Guy Arab IV chassis with new-look front and the chassis frame stretching to the rear axle and beyond.

Above: Metro-Cammell worked to reduce the weight of its metal-framed bodies and this 1940 body for Coventry Corporation, for mounting on a Daimler COA6 chassis, shows how simple the structure of a bus body could be. Metro-Cammell's metal-framed structure was regarded as one of the most robust; the body structure in this case weighed just 2.4tons and the buses were 60-seaters, a high capacity for the time.

The finishing touches are added to RTW type Leyland Titan PD2s at the Leyland factory in 1949. These were London's first 8ft-wide double-deckers and were completely built at Leyland, unlike other members of the RT family that received bodies built in several parts of the country.

Below: A single-door Leyland Titan TN15 is constructed at the Park Royal works in London – traditional coachbuilding methods applied to a very advanced bus. Titan production would move from Park Royal to Workington in 1981.

Right: Double-deckers require to be tilted, unsupported, to 28deg, to prove their stability, and this is RM1, the first London Transport Routemaster, undergoing the test at London Transport's Aldenham Works in 1956.

New looks
The early 1950s

As the bus industry scrabbled to get hold of new buses in the postwar period to replace their worn-out prewar buses and rather basic wartime acquisitions, a whole host of small bodybuilders appeared looking to establish themselves in the market. Some were firms that had been involved in aircraft and other wartime production, and others had a railway background, while some were general bodybuilders who saw an opportunity in buses. Not all of their products were particularly well-built nor would many win any prizes for looks, but such was the desperation that even major bus operators turned to small, often local firms.

Not all of these bodies were service buses as some of the newcomers concentrated on coaches and those that built bus bodies didn't necessarily build on new chassis as these were in short supply anyway, but made a living by rebodying prewar chassis or refurbishing prewar and wartime vehicles.

As the situation eased, most of the newcomers dropped out of bus bodybuilding and a hard core of suppliers emerged. There were always a handful that dominated the market and typically supplied bodies to operators throughout the UK, and others that tended to concentrate on winning more localised business.

Leyland, Metro-Cammell and Park Royal were the three major bus bodybuilders with the capacity to supply large orders for a range of customers. Important, but often with more localised customers, were Alexander, East Lancs, Northern Counties, Roe and Willowbrook, while Burlingham and Duple, essentially luxury coach builders, also produced bus bodies. Other smaller builders included Beadle, Massey and Strachans.

AEC and Park Royal built this prototype Regal IV in 1949 to the still-current 27ft 6in length and used it as a demonstrator to various major operators, including London Transport, whose green livery it wears here. The 40-seat body styling owes something to the prewar AEC 5Q5 types built by Park Royal, and the wind-down half-drop side windows are clearly London-inspired. The overall effect is neat and businesslike, with only the swept mouldings behind each axle harking back to typical prewar design flourishes.

Leyland's first commercially-available underfloor-engined model was the Olympic HR40 developed as an integral model with MCW. Like the Regal IV prototype, the first Olympics were built to 27ft 6in length, but a 30ft version was soon available. The high build and squareness of the body is partly helped by the heavy moulding running round the bus, in this case below floor level. This bus is also liveried for London Transport and carried Green Line fleetnames. Although the Olympic went on to be a successful export model, UK market customers preferred to buy chassis for bodying to their own specification and Leyland quickly introduced the Royal Tiger to meet this demand. This bus was built by Metropolitan Cammell at its factory at Elmdon in the West Midlands, but production home-market Olympics were built by Weymann, at Addlestone, Surrey.

The products of one major builder, Eastern Coach Works (ECW), were only available to state-owned companies that were controlled by the British Transport Commission since 1948, which as far as buses were concerned meant the Tilling and Scottish groups, railway-owned fleets in Yorkshire, and London Transport. In practice the majority of ECW's output went to Tilling and (from the mid-1950s) Scottish companies, plus some notable bodies for London Transport and for Sheffield Joint Omnibus Committee's B and C fleets, in which BTC had an interest.

There were relationships between certain bodybuilders and chassis builders. Park Royal and Roe were recent members of the ACV Group, with chassis builders AEC, Crossley and Maudslay; ECW bodies were largely built on chassis built by Bristol, also state-owned; Metro-Cammell Weymann (MCW), a marketing umbrella for the Birmingham-based Metro-Cammell Carriage & Wagon company and Weymanns, based at Addlestone, Surrey, was developing a relationship with Leyland. Although buses were often referred to as MCW-bodied, we have tried to distinguish the products of the two factories so you will find references to both Metro-Cammell and Weymann bodies. In the 1960s the Addlestone factory of Weymann closed down and Metro-Cammell Weymann, MCW, became the manufacturer, based near Birmingham, and the MCW product range would change greatly in the 1970s.

The most significant newcomer was Saunders of Beaumaris, on the Isle of Anglesey, which won important export and London Transport business and, as Saunders-Roe, went on to develop lightweight alloy designs before its bus bodybuilding activities stopped in 1954.

Leyland had built bus bodies for many of its own chassis since its early days and while in 1950 this was a significant business in 1954 Leyland suddenly stopped building bodies. It had already worked with MCW on the integral Olympic single-decker and would briefly liaise with Saunders-Roe, returning to MCW as its main collaborator.

A few names from the roll-call of bodybuilders who grasped the postwar opportunity were still in business in 1950, but one by one they dropped by the wayside as the demand for new buses eased and they often returned to their core business activities. Significant names in bus as distinct from coach building that were still around in 1950 included Brockhouse, Brush, Lydney and Northern Coachbuilders.

Technical advances and a relaxed approach to vehicle dimensions eased the way for many of the design advances of the 1950s. Until 1950 two-axle single-deck buses and coaches could be up to 27ft 6in (8.38m) long and double-deckers 26ft (7.92m). These regulations were relaxed in 1950 to allow 30ft (9.14m) single-deckers and 27ft (8.22m) double-deckers. Until 1946 7ft 6in (2.28m) had been the maximum permitted width for a bus or coach; from that date buses could be up to 8ft (2.43m) wide, initially with the permission of the local Traffic Commissioner.

The biggest technical advance was the appearance of the underfloor-engined single-decker. AEC and Leyland, among others, had experimented by developing horizontal versions of their normal vertical engine types to enable them to fit under the (admittedly rather high) floor of buses and coaches, releasing the entire interior space for passenger-carrying. These designs went on the back-burner when war broke out but it was clear that there would be further development work in the postwar years.

It fell to Midland Red to put underfloor-engined buses into squadron service. Midland Red, the Birmingham & Midland Motor Omnibus Co Ltd to give it its full name, started building its own chassis in 1924 and in the late 1930s and during the war experimented with rear-engined and then underfloor-engined single-deckers. By 1946 it was able to start production of its BMMO S6 model and 100 were built, followed by the wider S8 and similar S9 and S10 types; by 1950, when other manufacturers were still getting their act together, Midland Red had over 450 underfloor-engined single-deckers in service.

Bodybuilders quickly came to terms with 30ft-long underfloor-engined single-deckers, though some operators were tempted to try different entrance and exit layouts. An early experiment with entrance positions was carried out by Swindon Corporation when it bought four of these Daimler Freelines with Park Royal 34-seat centre entrance standee-type bodies in 1953. The body has fewer Park Royal characteristics, and the deep side windows have been designed to allow standing passengers to see out of the bus. The use of a heavyweight chassis means that the unladen weight was 7.6tons, much the same as many contemporary double-deckers.

The first generally-available underfloor-engined single-deck buses were not built by one of the major companies, but by Sentinel, the Shrewsbury-based firm that was best-known for its steam wagons. Sentinel worked with the coachbuilder J C Beadle, of Dartford to produce the Sentinel-Beadle STC4, unveiled in 1948. Beadle had done some pioneering work on integrally-constructed buses where there was no separate chassis, had built buses around older mechanical units for various Tilling Group companies and would go on to produce coaches built around prewar double-deck chassis for BET Group firms.

The introduction of the lightweight STC4, which won orders from a number of operators – but most famously BET's Ribble company, sitting on Leyland's doorstep – probably spurred the others into action so that by 1950 a raft of underfloor-engined chassis was available. AEC, Dennis, Guy and Leyland had models available, with Albion, Atkinson, Bristol and Daimler following over the next couple of years.

Most manufacturers had gone down the heavyweight route producing solid big-engined chassis that with 30ft x 8ft bodies would weigh in at much the same as a double-decker. Unfortunately these appeared just at a time that fuel duty was increasing – it rose by over 300 per cent between 1950 and 1952 – and operators were realising that saving fuel was one financial

Above: Midland Red had done much pioneering work on underfloor-engined single-deckers in the early postwar years and by 1953, when this own-build BMMO S14 prototype was placed in service, it became the 600th underfloor bus in the fleet; most other operators were still dipping a nervous toe in the water at this time. Midland Red buses had a distinctive look that was not unattractive. Note the prominent water filler cap below the rather shallow front windscreen and the shaped wheelarches. The S14 was an integrally constructed bus with rubber suspension, independent at the front, disc brakes on all wheels and single wheels at the rear. This bus weighed in at a remarkable 4.95tons. The S14 went into production in 1954 and more than 200 would be built.

Right: The standard Tilling Group single-deck bus from 1952 to 1957 was the Bristol/ECW LS (Light Saloon), an integral-construction bus that made extensive use of light alloy in the underframe and body. All ECW bodies of this time had a clear family resemblance, largely a result of the style of glazing and a close attention to detail. This 1955 LS for Southern National shows the attractive lines, with high-set side windows, a deep driver's windscreen with three-part destination display above, and the plain front with low-set headlamps and a discreet Bristol Eastern Coach Works badge. ECW-bodied buses often looked heavier than they actually were;' this 45-seat bus weighed 6.35tons.

economy they should make. Soon they would be clamouring for lighter buses but those first underfloor-engined types were giving operators experience of this new layout and bodybuilders the chance to adapt their design and building skills to what was essentially a box shape.

Midland Red's look on its early postwar BMMO S types was pleasantly rounded, with gently curving front windscreens above a deep slatted grille with high-set headlamps and a fairly prominent fuel filler cap. The filler cap would remain but the body style gradually evolved. The first versions were 27ft 6in long, then came 8ft wide and 30ft long versions. The Midland Red single-deck look was characterised by the high-set, shallow side windows, a feature that could still be detected in the company's last 'home-made' single-deckers in 1970. Although Midland Red designed the bodies for its S type single-deck buses, these were built by a range of companies – including Brush and Metro-Cammell in the early days, and Plaxton and Willowbrook in later days, as well as Midland Red itself.

Beadle's bodywork for the Sentinel-Beadle STC4 had some characteristics in common with the Midland Red designs, with curved lower windscreen edges, a front-mounted radiator and filler-cap and a prominent grille. The STC4 was followed in 1950 with the six-cylinder STC6, 30ft-long and with a much more dramatic front end that didn't quite seem to match the rest of the body.

Then the big boys entered the fray. Brush built a few bodies on underfloor chassis before it pulled out of bus work, but the remaining mainstream builders quickly established their own designs.

MCW had worked with Leyland to produce the integral Olympic in 1948 and that general body style would be built for the next dozen or so years. Leyland had long been trying to convince the UK bus industry of the benefits of integral construction, though the general preference for separate body-on-chassis buses would persist for another 20 years. It also wanted to persuade operators that one-stop shopping was good for them. With its own in-house bodybuilding department this was clearly possible, but long after this closed it would achieve this with models like the National, Lynx and Titan.

Although the Olympic was Leyland's initial underfloor-engined single-decker, operators still wanted chassis that could be bodied by their preferred suppliers. So Leyland introduced the Royal Tiger to fulfil this demand.

Park Royal built some prototype bodies on AEC Regal IV chassis in 1949/50, but was heavily involved in export activities and double-deck work which meant that it was a couple of years before a distinct look appeared. Indeed its early prototypes had more than a hint of the prewar London Transport 5Q5 design about them.

London Transport chose the AEC Regal IV with Metro-Cammell bodywork as its standard single-decker for the 1950s and 700 RF types were built between 1951 and 1953, a mixture of Green Line coaches and buses for the Central and Country Areas. This is the first Central Area bus as delivered, with seats for 40 passengers and weighing 7.75tons. These solid buses benefited from LT's thorough approach to design matters, and the plain lines and red livery have been relieved by the LT roundel on the front panels and the relief colour band running round the windows. The body design was unique to LT, and although this example has its entrance mounted ahead of the front axle, it has no door as the Metropolitan Police would not allow these to be fitted to Central Area buses at the time.

Some of Park Royal's earliest orders from UK operators were for two-door or centre-entrance bodies with extra standing space for municipal customers, but the appearance of the prototype lightweight integral AEC/Park Royal Monocoach in 1953 introduced a style that would be built until 1960. With a deep roofline and a simple but attractive front end, this was probably one of the most successful designs of its time. It was built on AEC Monocoach underframe but, like Leyland, AEC soon discovered that operators wanted chassis, so the Reliance was introduced and carried this body, as did Leyland chassis. The winged moulding under the front windscreen, designed to incorporate an AEC badge, was a feature of many of these bodies.

Although Roe was Park Royal's sister company in the ACV Group it developed its own body styles for underfloor-engined chassis, though when all-metal bodies were required, rather than Roe's traditional composite (metal/wood) construction, Park Royal-design bodies were supplied. Single-deckers typically represented a small proportion of Roe's output.

Alexander's first bodies on underfloor-engined chassis were coaches and it would be 1955 before a standard single-deck bus body design emerged. Duple, which concentrated on coach bodies, built a small number of bus bodies on underfloor-engined chassis, and Burlingham, again principally a coach builder, produced a distinctive bus body during the 1950s.

Leyland had not built single-deck bodies since the war, but produced a design for its Royal Tiger chassis in 1951. This was a shallow-roofed, solid body that seemed to lack the flair that was normally associated with Leyland bodies. Like many of the contemporary bodies, it had a substantial moulding running round the bus at floor level.

ECW built its first body on Bristol LS underfloor-engined underframe in 1950, and this integral bus was in production between 1952 and 1958. The

Leyland's own-build body for its Royal Tiger chassis was by common consent not the most aesthetically pleasing of the designs on early underfloor single-deckers. The high waistline and shallow roof emphasise its high-built nature. This is a 1953 delivery for Cumberland, which by that time was part of the state-owned Tilling Group, but which was still receiving previously-ordered Leylands. Its weight is 7.6tons.

body had a clear ECW look with a flat front and low-mounted headlamps and the result was an attractive and functional bus that was familiar in many parts of England and Wales. It was available only to state-owned companies and apart from one small batch for Scottish Bus Group the vast majority went to Tilling Group companies.

London Transport, which had prompted so much pioneering work on alternative engine positions, bought 700 AEC Regal IV to its own specification between 1951 and 1953. The bodies were built by Metro-Cammell and bore the clear stamp of London Transport as they were handsome with a close attention to detail. There was no obvious similarity to MCW's contemporary Hermes body design and no RF type bodies were supplied to other operators.

Double-deckers too were going through a metamorphosis in 1950. Nothing quite as dramatic as the effect of underfloor engines but significant nonetheless. What had been on offer in the early years after the war was a mix of upgraded prewar or wartime chassis, often with bodywork that owed more to the 1930s rather than the 1940s. And in 1950 all that was going to change.

For a start, more sophisticated chassis were becoming available. AEC's big-engined Regent III, firstly to London Transport RT specification and then to 'provincial' spec, was gaining ground; Albion's CX37 Venturer had replaced the CX19; Crossley's DD42 series of chassis were a new postwar design; Daimler's CV series was a postwar version of its CO and CW chassis; the Dennis Lance was supplied in small numbers in the decade after the war; Foden had a serious stab at the double-deck market with the PVD6 from 1947; Guy's Arab III and IV were updated versions of its rugged wartime models; Leyland's big-engined Titan PD2 had replaced the stopgap PD1 model by 1950. Daimler also marketed a more sophisticated model, the CD650, but this never really found favour.

London's double-deck standard was the RT family, which would grow to nearly 7,000 buses on chassis built by AEC and Leyland with broadly similar – and sometimes interchangeable – bodywork by a range of builders.

Bristol, supplying only to the state-owned fleets by this stage, offered the longer, wider KSW version of its long-running K type, but with ECW had developed one of the most important bus models of all time, the Lodekka. Where previously double-deck buses on routes passing under low bridges had been built to the awkward upper deck side-gangway lowbridge layout, the Lodekka used a drop-centre rear axle to offer

normal seating on both decks within the height of 13ft 6in (4.11m). The Lodekka concept would be picked up by other builders but these would be nothing like as successful.

Midland Red, the other major company developing its own buses, had developed the BMMO D5, which was built in 1949/50 and shared a Midland Red look with its contemporary S series single-deckers. What caught the eye was the full-width bonnet and concealed radiator, a feature that many operators felt would make their buses look more modern although there were some bus companies that stuck to exposed radiators right to the bitter end.

Midland Red had pioneered what became known as 'new-look fronts' in 1944 on its prototype BMMO D1 but Foden was first on the open market, in 1947, with its distinctive front end, based on its truck designs. Midland Red followed with its AD2 type double-deckers, based on AEC Regent II and delivered in 1948. Its close neighbour, Birmingham City Transport, decided to develop its own new-look front, which ended up halfway between an exposed radiator and a full-width front but was specified on Crossley, Daimler and Guy chassis. Daimler and Guy, and even briefly AEC, offered this style on chassis on the open market and later Dennis fitted a version of it to some Lance K4 chassis for Aldershot & District.

Bristol's two prototype Lodekkas had exposed radiators, admittedly very wide radiators in the style of the Daimler CD650, but production versions had fronts that were wider versions of the new-look style.

The lighter-weight chassis that appeared in 1952/53 were a response to concerns among operators about high weight and its effects on fuel consumption. AEC's main offering was the Reliance, which would remain on the model lists until 1979. This Reliance with Weymann-built MCW Hermes 44-seat bodywork weighs 5.9tons and was one of a batch of 40 delivered to BET's Potteries fleet in 1955. This basic body shape would serve MCW well for over a decade and became familiar in many parts of the country.

AEC and Leyland, the market leaders, held back to establish their own distinct frontal styles. AEC adopted an attractive design of front end that incorporated a stylised AEC radiator, but Leyland rather copped out and standardised on a front that had been developed for 100 Titan PD2s delivered to Midland Red specification.

Double-deck construction methods were changing too. There were more metal-framed bodies around and while most of these used steel, ECW was pioneering the use of aluminium alloy that would be adopted by most bus builders over the next 30 years. The London RT with its sleek lines and four-bay window layout (four window bays between the lower deck bulkheads) was causing bodybuilders and operators to look for something more 'modern'. It could be done simply by changing the glazing to a rubber-mounted style that allowed rounded corners to the windows or it could be done with a more fundamental rethink of design.

Some bodybuilders had already reached this stage by 1950. Roe had led the way with four-bay construction with its 1937 Commercial Motor Show exhibit on AEC Regent chassis for Leeds City Transport and in 1948 produced an updated version on Regent III for the same customer, creating a definite Roe 'look' that would survive in production until 1968.

Park Royal, not unreasonably, updated its double-deck range in 1950 with bodies that owed a great deal to the London RT and this look would see it through to the late 1950s.

Alexander jumped from bodies that owed a lot to Leyland styling to its own sleek four-bay designs in 1950, a basic shape that would continue in production until the late 1960s.

Metro-Cammell was kept busy building bodies to operators' specifications while Weymann had developed a restrained four-bay style that was chosen by several operators in preference to Metro-Cammell's 1952 offering, the Orion. Metro-Cammell was a pioneer of steel-framed bus bodies and had worked on high-capacity lightweight double-deckers for Coventry Corporation in the late prewar period. Now, understanding the appetite for lightweight buses, it introduced the Orion in 1952, where the body weighed little more than 2.5 tons (2267kg), allowing full-sized double-deckers to weigh in at little more than 6.5 tons (5896kg).

The downside for many operators and other observers was that the Orion looked like a lightweight bus, with no concessions, inside and out, to the features that people had come to expect. From the outside the deep lower deck windows and shallow upper deck windows looked unbalanced, though liveries could disguise this, and inside some operators eschewed interior lining panels and accepted single-skin roof domes to keep the weight down.

The trouble initially was that the chassis manufacturers had not always gone down the weight-saving route, but soon most had introduced slimmed-down versions of their standard double-deck models. AEC's Regent V, introduced in 1954, was one of these, as was BMMO's D7, Daimler's CL and pared-down CV series, and later Leyland Titan PD2s.

So while in 1950 many double-deck buses still looked rather as they had before the war, perhaps with rubber-glazed windows or a new-look front to give them a more 'modern' appearance, the moves to reduce body weight led to designs that are now clearly identified with the 1950s. The London RT design and the smoother looks pioneered by Midland Red were influencing other builders, but some stuck to a more gentle evolution. Northern Counties and Roe continued the subtle development of their mainstream body styles, giving their products a solid, timeless appearance. ECW's body for the Bristol Lodekka was identifiably a Lowestoft product, but with deep windows that gave the lowheight bus a pleasingly balanced look.

Big municipal fleets that had developed their own individual looks tended to stick to these in the early postwar period. The Birmingham City Transport standard design could still trace its ancestry to prewar buses, although the new-look front resulted in an interesting combination of traditional and modern design features. Manchester's distinctive streamline look survived into the postwar era in a toned-down form, but Manchester drifted towards what were largely standard bodybuilders' products while Birmingham, as a result of massive postwar fleet investment, bought no new double-deckers between 1955 and 1960.

The changes around 1950 helped create a healthier bus industry but there was still a demand for longer buses and when that came in 1956 the shape of double-deck buses was set to change for ever.

With the postwar push for bigger buses, distinct designs built for lightly-loaded, often rural, bus routes were low on the priority list. Before the war models like the Dennis Ace and Leyland Cub gave operators small, fairly basic models for such services, but these buses were needing replacement and the major manufacturers had little to offer. Even Bedford, which had built its business on smaller models like the legendary OB, could only offer adapted goods chassis when companies like David MacBrayne came looking for buses for deep rural operation.

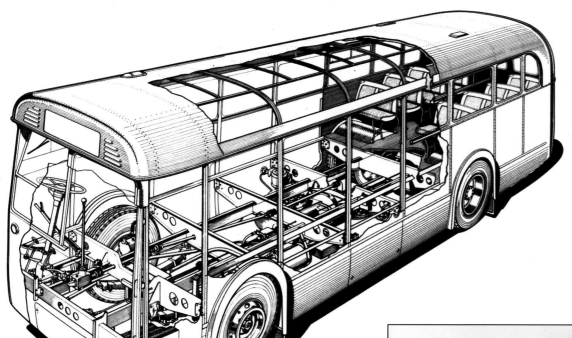

When London Transport needed smaller buses to replace its ageing Leyland Cubs it turned to Guy in 1953, who produced a special version of its Vixen chassis, and these were fitted with ECW bodywork. The resulting GS type buses were attractive and functional buses.

ECW also bodied the Bristol SC4LK, introduced in 1954, which was adopted by Tilling Group fleets needing smaller buses. While the GS type was to normal control layout, with the driver behind the engine, the SC4LK was a full-fronted forward control model.

In 1954 Aldershot & District turned to its favoured chassis supplier, Dennis, to produce the P5, a normal control version of its Falcon chassis, to which Strachans bodies were fitted.

The only other attempt to produce a custom-built small bus – what today would be classed as a midibus – was Albion, now under Leyland control, whose 1955 Nimbus was an underfloor-engined chassis. It offered bodybuilders the chance to build scaled-down versions of their usual designs, but some later versions were singularly attractive.

AEC and Park Royal, both partners within the ACV Group, dabbled in integral buses with the Monocoach and this is the 1953 prototype, which was painted in Green Line colours and demonstrated to London Transport. The weight, 5.4tons, was some 30 per cent less than the London RF type. The body has some London touches, and the shape of the front windows was a feature that was found on some of the earliest underfloor buses before straight lower edges became standard. The decorative mouldings above the AEC badge would be transformed into a winged motif on production Monocoaches. London bought no similar buses, and the main Monocoach customer was Scottish Bus Group. The cutaway drawing shows how the body structure was integrated with the crossmembers of the underframe, and the horizontal engine mid-mounted within the wheelbase.

Above: Coachbuilders like Burlingham, Duple, Harrington and Plaxton tended to concentrate on luxury coach bodies during the winter months to make sure operators received their new coaches by Easter each year and would often fill in the summer period by building batches of service bus bodies. Burlingham, based in Blackpool, developed a readily-recognisable single-deck bus body style, with heavily-radiused side windows and a decorative flash on the front panels. This is a 1954 Leyland Tiger Cub with 44-seat Burlingham body delivered to Baxter's of Airdrie, a well-regarded independent that tended to buy new vehicles for its services. Although it is basically similar to many other contemporary single-deckers, Burlingham has managed to produce a distinctive and attractive design.

Left: J C Beadle of Dartford was involved in bodywork for the pioneering Sentinel single-deckers as well as producing integral coaches for BET Group companies built around older mechanical units. By the mid-1950s it was offering a range of new-build integral vehicles using Commer mechanical units. Many were coaches but there was also the Beadle Chatham 45-seat bus, one of the more distinctive designs of the time with its distinctive windscreens featuring heavily-radiused outer top corners. This example went to Yorkshire Traction in 1956, and weighed 5.5tons.

Right: There was much emphasis in the 1950s on maximum-capacity full-size buses and few manufacturers had products on their lists when operators called for smaller buses. The option for London Transport was to develop its own bespoke buses and the solution was a special version of the normal control Guy Vixen chassis, with a Briggs bonnet of the type used on Ford Thames trucks. Taking advantage of its involvement in the British Transport Commission it developed a body with Eastern Coach Works (ECW), and the resulting GS type was a smart and practical 25ft-long 26-seater for Country Area work. London Transport has managed to retain its quality appearance on these unusual buses, which are an interesting combination of LT and ECW thinking. They weighed exactly 4tons.

Left: The Tilling Group's answer to the need for low-cost lightweight smaller buses for rural work was the Bristol SC with 35-seat ECW bodywork. The SC was never the prettiest of buses but it had the advantage of a well-built and spacious body. The Gardner 4LK engine was mounted at the front, beside the driver. Eastern Counties was a major customer for the SC and a total of 327 SCs were built between 1954 and 1962. The bus photographed weighed just over 4tons.

This was the design that in many ways set the standard for post-World War 2 double-deckers, the iconic London Transport RT. The design had been born just before the war, but mass deliveries started in 1947 and continued until 1954 by which time the RT family, on AEC and Leyland chassis, totalled nearly 7,000 buses. The proportions of the RT are near-perfect, with LT's usual awareness of good design and attention to detail. The lower-set radiator helps to tidy up the cab front area, a part of the bus that sometimes didn't work on other designs, and gives the driver excellent forward vision. This classic official photo against St Paul's Cathedral, shows the RT off to good advantage. Park Royal and Weymann built the majority of the bodies, which were designed to be interchangeable to take account of LT's overhaul procedures; the bus shown was new in 1952 with a Weymann body. Other RT family bodies were built by Cravens, Saunders and Metro-Cammell, and by Leyland for the 8ft-wide RTW type. The Cravens and Metro-Cammell bodies were not interchangeable with bodies of other makes, nor of course were the wider Leyland bodies.

Right: One of the main design features of the RT body design was the adoption of a four-bay window layout, with four side windows on the lower deck between the front and rear bulkheads. Roe had introduced a four-bay body in 1937 for Leeds City Transport, where previously five-bay and even six-bay layouts were common, and LT picked up on this arrangement, which gave bodies a sleeker and less fussy look. Park Royal offered four-bay bodies on AEC Regent chassis in the early postwar period, and later adopted designs that had more than a touch of the RT about them. Its new standard double-deck metal-framed body, introduced in 1950, was clearly inspired by the RT, and this can be seen clearly on this Guy Arab III for East Kent, one of 40 delivered in 1951. Although the higher-set Guy radiator sits less comfortably with the front end that the London RT, the overall effect is satisfying – though the bus is heavy at 8.2tons.

Right: In shape and outline Leyland's postwar bodywork was still recognisably developed from the 1938 metal-framed design built on Titan TD5 chassis. From 1950 until Leyland stopped building bus bodies this was the double-deck offering, with a revised style of glazing and a timeless appearance. Leyland still stuck to five-bay bodies, and on 8ft-wide examples like this 1954 58-seat delivery to Stockton Corporation the body tapered inwards from behind the front axle to allow the same front windows to be fitted to both 7ft 6in and 8ft widths. This is what was referred to as a highbridge bus – one with normal seating on both decks and an overall height of around 14ft 6in. Like most builders, Leyland also offered a lowbridge version, up to 1ft lower, with an offside sunken gangway and four-across seating on the upper deck.

Left: One of the more amazing confections of the early 1950s was the Roe double-deck coach bodywork built on Leyland Titan PD2 chassis for East Yorkshire in 1951. The 50-seat bodies featured ornate full-width fronts, extra brightwork on the body sides, and the contoured roof that was specified for many East Yorkshire double-deckers to allow them to pass through the Beverley Bar. Walsall Corporation took Leyland PD2s in 1953 with similar full-front bodies, but with four bays, normal roofs and deeper windscreens.

Left: While many operators rebuilt their utility double-deckers or sent them to specialist coachbuilders for this work, others chose to have what were sound chassis fitted with completely new bodies. This 1944 Guy Arab II of Yorkshire Traction went to Roe in 1952 to receive this new 56-seat body to Roe's standard composite style, complete with the distinctive pear-shaped window at the rear of the lower deck, helping to illuminate the staircase. The front-end styling with a flat dash panel, and what could be Leyland mudwings and headlamps, give this bus a distinctive look.

Right: An even more drastic rebodying exercise was carried out by Edinburgh Corporation, which bought 60 former London Transport Guy Arabs in 1952, rebuilt the chassis to 8ft wide and contracted Duple/Nudd to build new lightweight bodies on them. The full front design, with a decorative front hiding the Guy radiator, is interesting in that the nearside 'screen' is unglazed and the access to the bonnet above the front wheel was also open. This 55-seater, with the minimum of opening windows, weighed 6.65tons.

CITY & ROYAL BURGH OF EDINBURGH
W M LITTLE, *Transport Manager*

Below: While the last RT types were still being built, London Transport was developing a new design that would be used to replace LT's large trolleybus fleet. The prototype Routemaster was first shown in 1954 and is seen here in 1956 in the form it first entered service. Although the body layout was conventional, with seats for 64 passengers rather than the 56 of the RT, it was longer, wider and lighter than the RT. To the casual observer the RM may have looked like a modernised RT, but under the skin it was a very different and very advanced bus. It was integrally constructed, with no chassis, and the running units were attached to an aluminium alloy body. Automatic transmission, power-assisted steering and independent front suspension were just some of the mechanical advances. RM1, seen here, shows the more upright front end and deeper side windows, as well as the novel lower front-end styling. An underfloor-mounted radiator meant that no radiator grille as such was needed, and so LT came up with this design, incorporating the familiar roundel. When the radiator moved to its more conventional front-mounted position, bulbous grilles were grafted on to the prototypes, though production models benefited from a neater layout.

Above: Birmingham City Transport had clear ideas about double-deck bus design and invested in large fleets of broadly standard vehicles. The postwar Birmingham look first appeared in 1947 and similar five-bay bodies were built by a range of firms on a range of chassis types until 1954. Local firms Daimler and Metro-Cammell supplied most, but chassis were also bought from Crossley, Leyland and Guy, and bodies from Brush and Crossley, and just one, shown here, from Saunders-Roe. The early Birmingham deliveries had exposed radiators, but in 1950 this style of 'new-look' front was developed and fitted to Crossley, Daimler and Guy chassis. Birmingham City Transport's near-neighbour, Midland Red, had standardised on full-with fronts concealing the radiators from its first postwar deliveries in 1946 and this may have prompted the municipal operator to follow suit, but the BCT style retained separate mudwings and simply enclosed the radiator and engine compartment, with the headlamps mounted either side of simple vertical grille openings. Several manufacturers went on to adopt this style as their standard new-look front, notably Daimler and Guy, though some AEC and Dennis chassis also used similar fronts. The Birmingham-style body was designed to suit BCT's dark blue/cream livery, with heavy mouldings around the upper deck panelling, heavy upper deck front corner pillars and the recessed driver's windscreen. This is the solitary Guy Arab IV with Saunders-Roe 55-seat bodywork, and although regarded as a lightweight bus it still weighed in at 7.2tons. By 1954, when construction of this style of body ceased, it was looking slightly anachronistic compared with the lighter and simpler bodies entering service elsewhere in the UK.

The Stirling coachworks of Walter Alexander had developed as a sideline for the important bus-operating business, and before World War 2 most of its production went to companies in the SMT Group. When that group went into state-ownership in 1949 the coachworks stayed with the Alexander family and its customer base gradually widened until it became one of the UK's leading bodybuilders. The Scottish Bus Group continued to buy Alexander bodies, though it could – and did – buy Bristol and ECW products as part of the British Transport Commission. SBG also needed lowheight double-deckers like this 1956 Guy Arab IV with 59-seat Alexander lowbridge body, complete with rear platform doors. The attractive and well-balanced body was not unlike contemporary Northern Counties deliveries to group companies, right down to the heavily radiused outer corners of the upper deck front windows. The triangular destination box became a standard fitting on SBG double-deckers from around this time, though it had been pioneered by Ribble in 1947.

Right: Another new-look Guy Arab IV, this time for Sunderland Corporation with Crossley bodywork and dating from 1954. Crossley, along with AEC, Park Royal and Roe, was part of the ACV Group, and the body has a Park Royal look. On this bus the lower saloon pillars were of steel and the upper saloon pillars of aluminium alloy, and the weight was 7.15tons. The deep windows and the sloping front give the bus an attractive appearance.

Below: After supplying Regent III chassis with Birmingham-style new-look front to fleets including Bradford and Hull Corporations and the Devon General and South Wales company fleets, AEC developed its own design of full-width front incorporating a stylised version of the AEC radiator. The result was attractive, particularly when combined with stylish four-bay bodywork from Weymann. While Metro-Cammell at Elmdon was building the lightweight and much-derided Orion, Weymann was turning out more traditionally style bodies like this four-bay example for Rochdale Corporation. Although the blue/cream livery with its streamlined downsweep belonged to an earlier era, the overall effect oozed quality. At 7.8tons, this 61-seater was certainly no lightweight, when contemporary buses of the same size could be a full ton lighter.

Right: Leyland's full-width front first appeared on 100 Leyland Titans with Leyland bodies supplied to Midland Red in 1953, and was subsequently offered as an alternative to the traditional Leyland exposed radiator. Wider than the Birmingham-style front, it had a deep-slatted grille with space at the top that was originally designed for the BMMO insignia. Most operators, like St Helens Corporation here, used it for a badge or crest. Four newly-delivered Leyland Titans are seen in 1955, carrying 61-seat East Lancs bodies, built at Blackburn. The well-proportioned bodies suit the red/cream St Helens livery and the buses are well finished, right down to London-style rear wheel embellishers. These buses show how slightly recessed glazing can add to the feeling of quality.

Left: If there was one double-deck body that typified the desire for lighter buses in the 1950s it was the Metro-Cammell Orion, here in possibly its most notorious incarnations as one of the 300 Orions on Leyland Titan chassis delivered to Edinburgh Corporation in 1954-57 for tram replacement. Metro-Cammell had long experience of building metal-framed bodies, and in the late 1930s had developed an ultra-light body for Coventry Corporation. In 1952 it launched the Orion, a design that ignored previous conventions and in spite of its many detractors influenced body design for some time and actually proved to be robust and long-lived. The Edinburgh buses were very light – this 60-seater weighed just 6.6tons – and of this the body weighed just 2.25tons. The Edinburgh specification was fairly basic, to keep weight down, and features like the lack of opening windows other than at the front of each deck was remedied on subsequent batches. The fact that the lower deck windows were deeper than the upper deck ones was a notable feature of the Orion, perhaps accentuated by the application of Edinburgh's madder/white livery. It is interesting that on mainstream Orion bodies Metro-Cammell opted for a five-bay window layout rather than the currently more fashionable four-bay.

Above: Massey was a smaller coachbuilder based in Wigan, with loyal customers in the municipal and independent sectors. Its designs were normally pleasantly rounded and workmanlike. This is a 1956 AEC Regent V 58-seater, weighing just over 7tons, for Great Yarmouth Corporation. The body is to four-bay layout, though Massey also supplied five-bay bodies on other chassis.

Left: Contrasting with the Edinburgh Leyland is this rather more traditional Daimler CVG6 delivered to Halifax Corporation, also in 1954. The body is by Charles H Roe, part of the ACV Group. Roe continued to offer teak-framed composite wood/metal bodies long after most other builders had gone over to metal-framed construction. The striking green/orange/cream Halifax livery suits the restrained lines, with four-bay construction and a gently sloping front end. The inset glazing always gave buses a look of quality compared with the flush-mounted glazing of bodies like Metro-Cammell's Orion. Just visible below the lower deck windows is the distinctive Roe steel waistrail that distinguished its composite bodies from its metal-framed ones and gave extra strength to the body. Although Roe built an increasing number of metal-framed bodies, some to Park Royal design or using Park Royal frames, some customers preferred to order composite bodies until 1968. Like most Roe official photographs, the Halifax Daimler is seen outside the company's factory at Crossgates, Leeds.

Below left: Willowbrook bodywork for double-deckers was easily distinguished by the heavy upper deck front corner pillars, and on this 1955 demonstrator built for Daimler, the front upper windows are also recessed. This bus, registered SDU 711, was unusual in being built to a height of just 14ft, between the typical lowbridge and highbridge heights of the time. Willowbrook Ltd, based at Loughborough, had bought the bus bodybuilding business of Brush in 1952, and would itself be taken over by Duple in 1958, though the Willowbrook name survived for some years.

Below: Most of the smaller bodybuilders that had sprung up in the early postwar years to satisfy the demand for bodies on new and reconditioned chassis had moved away from bus work by the early 1950s, but one that kept going with small batches was Reading of Portsmouth, which built the 59-seat lowbridge bodies on two AEC Regent V for West Bridgford UDC in 1957. The effect was a competent, attractive and balanced four-bay body. West Bridgford was one of the small number of Urban District Councils in England and Wales operating their own bus fleets; West Bridgford UDC was sold to Nottingham Corporation in 1968.

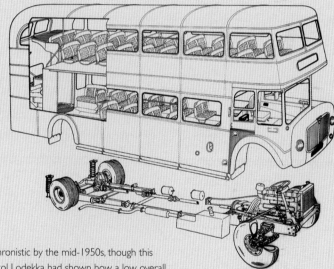

Side-gangway lowbridge buses like the West Bridgford AEC were becoming increasingly anachronistic by the mid-1950s, though this didn't prevent some operators from specifying them right through to the late 1960s. The Bristol Lodekka had shown how a low overall height and normal seating could be successfully combined, but of course Bristol and ECW products were only available to state-owned fleets at the time. It was probably inevitable that other manufacturers would look to develop equivalent products for the general market, and Associated Commercial Vehicles, ACV, the parent group that included AEC, Crossley, Park Royal and Roe, developed its own lowheight double-decker, the Bridgemaster. Development work was handled by Crossley, and the prototype carried a Crossley badge. It was one of the first double-deckers built to the newly-permitted 30ft length and was first shown at the 1956 Commercial Motor Show, the same event that Leyland chose to launch its new rear-engined Atlantean. The 72-seat prototype Bridgemaster weighed under 8tons, and featured an aluminium-framed body mounted integrally with a simple underframe with independent front suspension rather like the contemporary Routemaster. The body on the prototype, registered 9 JML as a demonstrator, was well-proportioned and attractive, with a clear impression that it had been designed as a whole. Production Bridgemasters would be steel-framed and Park Royal produced a less satisfactory body design for these.

The prototype 30ft-long Leyland/MCW Atlantean caused a sensation when it was launched in 1956, introducing a look that was revolutionary then but became familiar very quickly. The integral bus had styling that would stay unique, with a definite MCW look to the top deck, with an interesting lower front end with an oval device to get away from the potential blandness and an opening flat-glass driver's window with a separate curved-glass corner piece. The lowheight bus had equal-depth side windows on both decks and some slightly wider pillars that were largely structural. This bus was a 78-seat demonstrator.

Longer and lighter
The late 1950s

By 1956 lightweight buses were very much the flavour of the time. Single-deck models like AEC's Regal IV and Leyland's Royal Tiger continued as successful export models but the smaller-engined and lighter Reliance and Tiger Cub were the main home market models. Albion introduced a lighter version of the Tiger Cub, the Aberdonian; Atkinson introduced PL745H and PL746H models; Bristol continued with its LS; Dennis had the Lancet UF; and Guy produced the LUF version of the Arab. Daimler stuck with its heavyweight Freeline, but Midland Red had progressed through its S series to reach the S14, which broke new ground with its integral construction, stressed-skin body, independent front suspension and disc brakes – and weighed in at just 5.5 tons (4989kg).

One of the most iconic double-deckers of all time, the London Transport Routemaster, had appeared in prototype form in 1954, although it would be another five years before production versions would be seen on London's streets. In the intervening period, though, much had changed. The maximum dimensions for a two-axle double-decker were increased in 1956 to 30ft (9.14m) long and this prompted a stream of lengthened chassis from AEC, Bristol, Daimler, Guy and Leyland, as well as totally new models over the next five years from AEC, Albion, BMMO, Daimler, Dennis, Guy and Leyland.

The AEC, Albion and Dennis models were doubtless prompted by the success of Bristol's Lodekka with the state-owned fleets. Sensing an untapped market among in the BET and municipal markets for lowheight models, AEC introduced the Bridgemaster in 1956, Albion the Lowlander in 1961 and Dennis the Loline (a version of the Lodekka built under licence)

The prototype Leyland Atlantean created a huge impact in 1956 and when production models appeared in 1958 there was disappointment that these turned out to be rather less attractive. In the intervening two years Leyland had redesigned the Atlantean as a separate chassis and this was supplied with the engine contained within a one-piece cover. Initially this presented bodybuilders with a problem which they overcame with the layout at the rear of Wallasey Corporation's first Atlantean, Metro-Cammell-bodied, with the rear profile broken by a cutaway above the engine compartment. The sleek lines of the prototype gave way to a design reminiscent of the widely unloved Orion body, with unequal depth side windows. This was partly because Leyland was unable at the time to offer the Atlantean with a drop-centre rear axle to allow the type of bodywork seen on the prototype, so this normal height body was designed. The Wallasey sea green/cream livery helps to disguise the unbalanced lines, although the traditional municipal shaded lettering used for the fleetname seems at odds with such a modern bus. The uninspired flat lower front end suggests an opportunity missed and this body style set the Atlantean look for some years. It was a 30ft-long 78-seater.

The proportions of the Alexander body for the Atlantean were broadly those of the Metro-Cammell design, yet the deeper roof and the rounded front dome gave the buses a rather more pleasing appearance. This 1959 78-seater was supplied to Sunderland District, and is posed outside the bodybuilder's recently-opened coachworks at Falkirk.

in 1957. While the Lowlander and Loline were fairly conventional front-engined models with drop-centre rear axles, the Bridgemaster was an integral bus built in conjunction with Park Royal and featured coil spring suspension (later air), independent at the front. All three models found customers but none even came close to selling in the numbers that the Lodekka did.

The development process for the Routemaster was a long one, in true London Transport fashion, and when the prototype Routemaster was unveiled in 1954 its looks still owed much to the RT, updated and with a stylish full-width front. Mechanically, of course, the Routemaster represented a huge step forward, and even when it went into series production in 1959 it was still more advanced than most of the competition. The trouble was that it was conceived as a trolleybus replacement, and was designed as a conventional rear entrance bus when nobody could have anticipated the spread of driver-only operation to save

costs. A forward entrance version was designed, but found little favour in London, and there was even a rear-engined version that may have been sacrificed at the altar of British Leyland.

Midland Red, as always, did its own thing. Its next double-deck model, the last that would go into series production, was the BMMO D9, which was bristling with new features – integral construction, rubber suspension that was independent at the front, disc brakes – and 344 were produced between 1958 and 1965. The body still had a definite Midland Red look but with a novel set-back front axle. Midland Red's last own-make double-deck, the D10, was underfloor-engined, and though only two were built, the idea would resurface in the Volvo D10M/Citybus and Leyland Lion, though high floorlines and the high centre of gravity would always legislate against this layout.

Guy's new 1959 model was the Wulfrunian, a front-engined chassis that had the entrance ahead of the front wheels. It had air suspension all round, independent on the front, and disc brakes, but while it sold largely to the then-independent West Riding company, it has come to be regarded as an expensive failure, contributing to the sell-offs of both Guy and West Riding.

It was Leyland's new model that changed the shape of double-deckers for ever. This was the Atlantean, first introduced in 1956 as a semi-integral bus with Metro-Cammell body, which defied convention by mounting the engine transversely across the rear. Feedback from operators caused Leyland to rethink the Atlantean, which then appeared in 1958 as a separate chassis and went on to be a hugely successful model, remaining in production until the 1980s.

Daimler followed Leyland's lead with the Fleetline in 1960 featuring a Gardner engine, which endeared it to many engineers, and a drop-centre rear axle to offer a proper lowheight layout; Leyland could only achieve this on early production Atlanteans with an awkward upper deck layout.

These new designs presented challenges and opportunities for bodybuilders. In the case of the front-engined lowheight chassis there was the problem of the essentially high-mounted engine compartment and driver's cab and the low build of the rest of the body, which some builders solved more successfully than others. But with the Atlantean and Fleetline, and to a degree with the Wulfrunian, builders faced the same challenge that they had with single-deckers around 1950 – making what was essentially a box look attractive.

There was one slight problem: they didn't succeed. The prototype Atlantean looked rather good and was certainly different from anything that

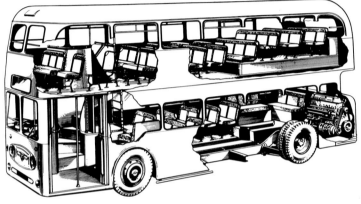

had been seen before. The main bodybuilder at the start was Metro-Cammell with Weymann handling the semi-lowbridge examples, and the designs built on early production Atlanteans seemed to be based on the controversial Orion design with unequal-depth windows on normal height examples, which was disappointing given the opportunities offered to designers by the shape. On the prototype Atlantean the engine compartment was enclosed within the body shape but on the production versions the engine compartment was a very obvious feature of the rear end and though it looked rather like an afterthought it was intended to provide easier access. Side fairings would soon give rear-engined double-deckers a smoother profile and much later models would revert to the enclosed engine of the Atlantean prototype.

Many operators were initially cautious about Atlanteans and Fleetlines, preferring to stick to tried and tested front-engined chassis for their purchases, though some went for the longer 30ft chassis now available and

Leyland offered a lowheight Atlantean with a slightly awkward upper deck layout with a partial side gangway towards the rear. Weymann built many of the lowheight Atlanteans like this 1958 bus for Maidstone & District. The front end is similar to the Wallasey bus, slightly helped by M&D's traditional 'wings' below the front windscreens. The deep lower deck windows of the normal height Atlantean have been replaced by equal-depth windows on both decks, which gives a more balanced appearance, but the body layout was never very popular. This 73-seat lowheight Atlantean weighed 8.6tons. A Leyland cutaway drawing released in 1958 shows how the low height of 13.12ft was achieved – though the front end is clearly based on the 1956 prototype rather than production buses.

others went for forward entrances, immediately behind the front axle. Forward entrance double-deckers were not new but their widespread adoption in the 1950s and 1960s represented the largest expression of interest in a layout that was often awkward and impractical.

Some operators wanted their new 30ft-long forward entrance double-deckers to be a bit different, with front ends that looked, perhaps, like the new-fangled Atlantean. The solution was to enclose the radiator and bonnet within a full-width front end. Ribble and Southdown, two of the biggest BET

Group fleets, developed recognisable designs. Both were based on Leyland Titan PD3 chassis; the Ribble design had Burlingham bodywork and Southdown turned to Northern Counties; later Ribble examples had Metro-Cammell bodies, though the overall effect was less successful.

Most of the longer double-deckers, though, looked like lengthened versions of their shorter brothers. Not all operators favoured forward entrances and stuck with rear entrances, sometimes with platform doors. Some 30ft double-deckers even had exposed radiators, specified by operators who preferred the ease of access that these offered. There were still operators choosing lowbridge bodies in preference to the lowheight buses on offer, and some of the last of this generation of front-engined double-deckers had exposed radiators or lowbridge bodies – in a few cases, both.

Single-deck buses continued to develop, with moves away from the square, high-waisted styles of the early 1950s, towards more curvaceous designs. BET Group, which had developed an attractive standard single-deck style in the 1930s was working on a new single-deck standard, which would develop over the next decade to become an all-time classic.

Above: Leyland's sectional drawing from 1956 shows the prototype integral Atlantean with its low build and sleek lines (it was only 13.23ft high), the enclosed engine compartment at the rear and the wide pillars behind the wheels.

Right: The ground-breaking Bristol/ECW Lodekka, built only for state-owned companies, was extended to 30ft long in 1957 and this Western National 70-seater was the first to be built, and it would be 1960 before 30ft-long production Lodekkas started to enter service. It has the basic shape of the original 1953 production Lodekkas, with the chunky Bristol new-look front, the shallow driver's windscreen and the gently sloping front-end profile. The use of equal-depth window on both decks gives the bus a balanced look, and the extra 3ft length has been quite neatly achieved by the use of a 'half-window' ahead of the rear platform; note the longer rear overhang. This bus weighed 8.35tons.

Far right: The 1956 Commercial Motor Show was the first opportunity for manufacturers to show examples of the newly-legalised 30ft-long double-deckers, and while some were advanced concepts like the Atlantean and Bridgemaster, others were simply lengthened versions of existing chassis, like this Potteries Leyland Titan PD3 with 74-seat MCW Orion bodywork. The body too is clearly little more than a lengthened version of the familiar 27ft Orion, and the six-bay window arrangement is interesting; most 30ft double-deckers – including Orions – would have five-bay bodies.

Left: Many operators took advantage of the extra length to sample forward-mounted entrances behind the front axle. Some operators stuck with this layout, while others reverted to rear-entrance buses. Some, after trying Atlanteans, even went back to front-engined buses. Contrasting with the 1956 Potteries Leyland PD3 is this 1959 delivery to South Wales Transport, an AEC Regent V with Orion-type body and a forward entrance 71-seat body built by Weymann at Addlestone. This benefits from a five-bay body with wider-spaced window pillars, although it shows this design at its starkest, as South Wales was one of a handful of operators that experimented with unpainted buses in an attempt to save costs and a little weight. The buses quickly tarnished, and tended to be painted in normal colours very quickly. This bus weighed 7.75tons.

Right: Massey lengthened its traditional body design to 30ft, as fitted to this 1958 Guy Arab IV for West Wales Motors of Tycroes. It carries a lowbridge body with rear-mounted platform doors and the sweeping lines of the body merge well with the Guy new-look front end. The trolleybus wires indicate that the photo was taken at Guy's hometown of Wolverhampton rather than in West Wales. It weighed 8.2tons.

Several larger operators sought to disguise their new double-deckers with full-width fronts, perhaps inspired by the appearance of the Leyland Atlantean. This (right) is a Ribble Leyland Titan PD3 with Burlingham 30-ft long 72-seat bodywork, and in place of an exposed radiator or full-width bonnet, Ribble has worked with the bodybuilder to produce a very satisfying full front with deep windscreens and a chrome-edged grille. The body has the usual heavily-radiused windows favoured by Burlingham, and the forward entrance has a one-piece sliding door rather than the inward-folding doors that would become more popular with many operators. Ribble later bought further similar PD3s with Metro-Cammell Orion-style bodies, but the direct glazing of the MCW body (left) seems to lack the solid look of the Burlingham equivalent. Other BET Group companies, notably East Kent and Southdown, opted for full fronts on their 30ft-long forward entrance double-deckers.

Left: Southdown also opted for a 30ft front-engined/forward entrance double-decker in the 1950s and 1960s, building up a substantial fleet of Northern Counties-bodied Leyland Titan PD3s between 1957 and 1967. They were all broadly the same as the bus shown here, a 1959 example, although there were variations to the lower front panel design, including buses with twin headlamps, with curved front screens on both decks, and with panoramic side windows. Like the Ribble buses, the front-end treatment is neat, and the 'half' window on the side will be noted; London Transport would adopt a similar feature when it produced its lengthened Routemasters in 1961. Note also the four-leaf inward folding doors, preferred by many operators over the sliding doors favoured by Ribble and East Kent. The Southdown PD3s were nicknamed 'Queen Marys'. This 69-seater weighed 8.15tons.

Above right: East Kent turned to AEC and Park Royal, regular suppliers to the company, for its 30ft double-deckers. These AEC Regent V with 72-seat bodies achieved the full front look by merging the normal AEC front end into the body structure, and the result, particularly with the well-balanced Park Royal gasket-glazed body, was very impressive. Again a sliding door has been specified and the bus weighed 8.4tons.

Left: The Dennis Loline was a Bristol Lodekka built under licence and available on the open market. The Loline front end went through different versions, but this 1958 version combines the proportions of the Lodekka with a Dennis grille and the bodywork on this bus for Walsall Corporation was built by Willowbrook. It features the distinctive Willowbrook heavy front upper deck corners but is otherwise well balanced. Again it uses a sliding door.

Below: The production AEC/Park Royal Bridgemaster looked rather different from its prototypes. The BET Group's requirement for steel-framed bodies resulted in a redesign that took away many of the good looks seen in the early buses and produced this more upright bus with rather less class. This is a 1960 Bridgemaster for South Wales Transport, a forward entrance 72-seater in an unrelieved red livery that did little to improve to looks of the bus.

Above: Edinburgh Corporation looked for something different for its first 30ft double-deck, and specified this Leyland Titan PD3 with 72-seat Alexander body, fitted with a Homalloy front in place of the Leyland full-width bonnets it had previously favoured. The distinctive fibreglass front end sat quite happily with the Alexander body, which was a lengthened version of a design that had been in production for a few years. The heavily curved upper deck first side windows were slightly at odds with the curve of the front end, but with equal-depth windows on both decks and folding doors, the effect was impressive. It weighed 8.05tons.

Right: Guy decided against following Leyland down the rear-engine route for its next double-deck model and instead produced the Wulfrunian, with its engine mounted at the front, squeezing the driver towards the offside wall and producing a narrow front platform, complete with nearside-mounted staircase. Mechanically, the Wulfrunian featured advanced features like independent suspension and disc brakes, but it could never be considered a success. Roe built most of the bodies for Wulfrunians, and this was a 1965 delivery to West Riding, which had been involved in the development of the model and became by far the principal customer. The 75-seat body has traces of Roe bodies on Leyland Atlanteans, and the nearside staircase over the front wheel, with a small triangular window, will be noted. Over a decade later, Volvo would revisit the front-engined layout with its considerably more successful Ailsa model.

Right: When the production version of London Transport's Routemaster appeared in the late 1950s, the overall lines were still the same but the front end appearance had changed. Some were disappointed when the rounded front end of RM1, shown on page 36, gave way to a design that incorporated the front-mounted radiator, but others prefer the purposeful look seen here, which still kept the sloping bonnet-top to give the driver excellent all-round vision, but incorporated a grille design that would prove to be timeless. This shows how the early Routemasters first appeared, and there would be subtle changes over the 10-year production run. This is the 27ft 6in long 64-seat Routemaster, weighing 7.25tons, but a 30ft-long 72-seat version would follow, by inserting a short window bay after the second full bay, and there were Green Line coach versions with doors and a forward entrance version, produced in both lengths. There was a prototype rear-engined Routemaster, the FRM, using a high proportion of common parts, but it was never allowed to develop.

Left: Deliveries of new trolleybuses slowed as the 1950s progressed and more systems were closed, but one customer was Glasgow Corporation, which was still replacing tram routes with trolleybuses. In 1957/58 it bought 90 of these BUT 9613T with 30ft Park Royal-design bodies built by Crossley. The very satisfying lines of the Park Royal design work well with the added length, and even the plain front end doesn't jar as it could do on other designs. This 70-seater weighed 8.5tons.

Below: The last new trolleybuses delivered to UK operators were Sunbeam MF2B with Weymann 63-seat bodies for Bournemouth Corporation in 1958-62. They featured the earlier style of Weymann body rather than the Orion-inspired designs that were coming out of the Addlestone factory and the result, with a simple but effective front end, was most attractive. The 30ft-long buses featured the traditional twin staircase layout favoured by Bournemouth.

Right: Daimler quickly designed a rear-engined double-deck chassis to compete with Leyland's Atlantean and in 1960 unveiled the Fleetline. The prototype was in Birmingham City Transport colours and carried a 72-seat MCW body built by Weymann, which was little different to the early bodies on Atlantean. Daimler too went for the enclosed rear engine compartment and the blandness of the lower front panels was broken up by the use of twin headlamps and a substantial fluted Daimler badge.

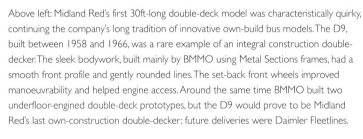

Above left: Midland Red's first 30ft-long double-deck model was characteristically quirky, continuing the company's long tradition of innovative own-build bus models. The D9, built between 1958 and 1966, was a rare example of an integral construction double-decker. The sleek bodywork, built mainly by BMMO using Metal Sections frames, had a smooth front profile and gently rounded lines. The set-back front wheels improved manoeuvrability and helped engine access. Around the same time BMMO built two underfloor-engined double-deck prototypes, but the D9 would prove to be Midland Red's last own-construction double-decker; future deliveries were Daimler Fleetlines.

Left: Through the 1950s the maximum dimensions for single-deckers stayed at 30ft × 8ft and Walter Alexander's first pure bus body for underfloor-engined chassis, apart from early prototypes, was this 1955 design, owing a little to Park Royal designs already in service with Scottish Bus Group companies, but with a shallower roof and distinctive, though slightly anachronistic, Alexander touches like the moulding above the side windows and the 'vee' created just ahead of the entrance door. Side mouldings under the windows are practical for painting, and a not unattractive flash between the headlamps takes away from a bland front. The recessed driver's windscreen was another popular feature of the time. This AEC Reliance, a 41-seater, was new to Scottish Omnibuses in 1957.

Left: There was a small continuing demand for lighter single-deckers, often for smaller operators or for non-PSV work. The Bedford/Duple combination had been a popular one since the 1930s and this is a 1958 SB with Duple metal-framed bodywork. Although it was a 42-seater, it weighed only 4.9 tons. The simple design marries the Bedford truck-style front with a rugged and businesslike body that features a fairly high waistline.

Right: In 1957 the semi-integral Bristol/ECW LS type bus was replaced by the similar MW, featuring a separate chassis. The ECW bodywork was changed to this design with deeper side windows, although still very obviously a Lowestoft product, and a more shapely front end incorporating a cooling grille. As with most Lowestoft products, the effect was competent and would quickly become familiar among Tilling Group fleets. This 41-seater was new in 1960 to Crosville. It retains the Bristol/ECW wing device of the LS and would be produced in express coach versions with rather more external brightwork and coach-type seats. A different body style was developed for 'proper' coaches. Over 1,000 MW buses were bodied by ECW between 1957 and 1965.

Below: By the late 1950s the main forces in the single-deck body market were Alexander, MCW, Park Royal-Roe and Willowbrook although builders of luxury coaches, notably Duple and Plaxton, and Harrington to a lesser extent, built service bus bodies in their quieter summer season. By this time a clear standard style was emerging, which would evolve into a style favoured particularly by BET Group companies. BET had standard designs in the years before and after World War 2, built by a range of bodybuilders. Now it was moving back to this situation, using its bulk-buying powers in the interests of standardisation. While Tilling Group companies had little or no choice in what they could buy, and Scottish Bus Group was largely standardising on Alexander products for its single-deck fleet, BET gave its managers a greater degree of choice in terms of chassis and body builders. Although they could – and did – buy a wide range of double-deck types, the single-deck choice for BET managers was largely down to a preferred chassis builder and a preferred bodybuilder, which still resulted in buses that looked broadly similar. This 1959 AEC Reliance with Park Royal 40-seat body, shows the clean businesslike lines, with deeper side windows than earlier underfloor-engined single-deckers, but still giving companies like Maidstone & District the opportunity to personalise the design with such features as the style of destination indicator, the mouldings above the side windows and the wing device on the front panelling. Note the large Pay As You Enter signs on the front and nearside, for around this time operators were able to operate larger single-deckers without a conductor and many eagerly chose this as a useful way to cut costs. This bus weighed 5.9tons.

Above: In time, Alexander too would be seduced by the possibility of custom from BET Group companies and would build to the standard design, but its main customers were still in Scotland, and it continued to develop body styles to suit the local market, SBG in particular. This design first appeared in 1957, a rather more rounded design than its earlier bus body, seen on page 57. This allowed SBG fleets to specify these as pure service buses or the dual-purpose types with coach-like seats beloved of company fleets. This 1961 example shows the gently curving lines and the sloping front end which was an antidote to the squared-off fronts of so many underfloor-engined single-deckers. This bus was for the independent operator, Carmichael of Glenboig, trading as Highland, and is mounted on an early example of a chassis that would go on to greater things, the Leyland Leopard. After years of hard-working small-engined types like the Leyland Tiger Cub, some operators were looking for beefier buses, so the big-engined Leopard was born. The body style has a number of recognisable Alexander features, including that 'vee' at the front roofline corner, and differed from the products of other builders with its centre-mounted offside emergency door, creating a half-bay in the window line. A 45-seater, it weighed 6.15tons.

A hint of things to come was given in 1958 when Glasgow Corporation obtained permission to operate single-deckers longer than the 30ft legal maximum. These were trolleybuses for a specific route and they were 34ft 5in long with seats for 50. Burlingham built the bodies on BUT RETB1 chassis and the result was sleek and low-built. The front of the body has strong Burlingham features, including the winged device, but the side windows lack the heavily-radiused style that was a Burlingham trademark for so many years.

Styling takes over
The 1960s

It took another major change in vehicle dimensions to signal the next major moves in UK bus design. From 1961 buses and coaches, single-deck and double-deck, could be up to 36ft (10.97m) long and 8ft 2½in (2.50m) wide. At 20 per cent longer, this was the greatest single increase in dimensions at any time in the history of motorbuses and manufacturers and operators were quick to embrace the new freedoms. While some slightly longer double-deckers appeared, the main attraction was for operators who wanted extra capacity in their single-deckers. Where 35 seats was a typical seating capacity in the days of 27ft 6in-long single-deckers, rising to 44/45 in 30ft underfloor-engined single-deckers, now 53 seats were possible, the same as many lowbridge double-deckers

AEC and Leyland were now the main suppliers of full-size single-deckers and introduced lengthened versions of their Reliance and Leopard chassis; the Leyland Leopard had been introduced in 1959 as a 30ft-long chassis, a larger-engined equivalent of its Tiger Cub.

These underfloor-engined models were the first 36-footers but the new dimensions were encouraging manufacturers to develop rear-engined single-deckers. Bristol got there first. Its integral LS had been replaced by the underfloor-engined MW chassis, but rather than a 36ft MW Bristol chose to go for a rear-engined chassis, the RE, that could be used as the basis for a bus or a coach.

The RE appeared in 1962 and was followed two years later by a range of other models. In 1962 AEC had been merged with its long-time rival, Leyland, and the chassis of their new 1964 models, the AEC Swift and Leyland Panther, shared many common parts. Daimler's offering was the Roadliner and used a Cummins V6 engine that proved to be unreliable and hastened the model's demise.

The 36ft-long models, underfloor-engined and rear-engined, gave bodybuilders the chance to introduce some important new designs which had their roots in a standard body designed for the BET Group and built by a range of companies. The BET Federation had produced single-deck designs in the 1930s and 1940s and bodybuilders were prepared to build to these designs because they were keen to win BET business. Designed as a 30ft model, the BET design grew first to slightly over the 30ft mark and then to 36ft. The first to the full length looked rather clumsy but soon an attractive front end was developed incorporating a curved windscreen and then the back was tidied up with a curved rear screen. Variations to this basic design would be built for the next dozen years and the BET style became a familiar sight throughout the country, far beyond the group's companies.

Another design that evolved from the BET design was the Alexander Y type. Alexander had designed bodies largely for Scottish Bus Group operators but had joined the list of suppliers to the BET Group and the Y type developed from bodies built for BET fleets. What marked the Y type out were the distinctive front and rear ends and, on many bodies, the forward-sloping panoramic side windows.

Some of the new design features were possible because of changes to legislation. Drivers no longer had to have opening windscreens, allowing

BET Group's requirement for steel-framed bodies and Park Royal-Roe's desire to use standard parts resulted in some unattractive confections in the early 1960s and surely one of the most ungainly bodies built on early rear-engined double-deckers was this style on Leyland Atlantean in 1960 for Trent. The lower deck windows are unusually high-set and the use of a standard top deck has created deep panelling between the windows, slightly exaggerated by the livery application. Designs like this may have prompted some operators to push for more attractive styling from the bodybuilders.

designers to create stylish looks using curved glass, and a wider adoption of glassfibre and other plastics allowed a more creative approach to curves and mouldings.

And just as single-deckers were getting a makeover, bus operators were forcing the pace with bodybuilders to improve the appearance of double-deckers. In place of the disappointingly bland designs that had emanated from MCW and Roe there appeared designs that were often associated with the operators who had first specified or at least influenced them. So Alexander produced a rounded style that was initially associated with Glasgow Corporation; Metro-Cammell did the same for Liverpool, Roe for

Leeds and Sunderland, Metro-Cammell and Park Royal for Birmingham, Park Royal for Sheffield, and East Lancs for Bolton. Nottingham developed a quirky style that would go on to be built by various companies until the mid-1980s. The ultimate own-design was Manchester's Mancunian, a body that had started with a clean sheet of paper and was the first double-decker designed specifically for driver-only operation, something that had been legalised in 1966.

This situation harked back to the days when Britain's major towns and cities had developed their own distinctive looks for their bus fleets. This welcome display of individuality certainly raised the bar as far as double-deck design was concerned and although some bland designs still slipped through there seemed to be a greater awareness of the importance of good design, which was also reflected in interior décor where passengers enjoyed bright and durable new materials rather than dark floral moquettes and polished wood.

Demands for better-looking buses that would attract passengers, together with the new materials that were available, led bodybuilders to look hard at what they offered, and they realised that little change was needed to the basic structure of their bodies and they could achieve significant improvements by concentrating on the front and back ends. Alexander did it with curved glass, which did not appeal to every operator as it can be expensive to replace, while other builders achieved equally impressive results by sticking to flat glass and adopting peaked domes. And rear ends could be improved by eliminating the engine compartment 'bustle' by fairing this in to create a smooth rear profile.

Manchester City Transport's Mancunian design started with a clean sheet of paper and represented as significant a development as its streamlined prewar namesake. It featured an extra-deep driver's windscreen and long side windows and looked clean and contemporary. Longer side windows were not new; Alexander and other builders had produced single-deck buses with panoramic side windows, a feature that had been pioneered on Plaxton coaches in the late 1950s, and Alexander had built panoramic-windowed double-deckers for Edinburgh Corporation from 1965, essentially replacing two smaller window bays with a longer one. The Mancunian took this one stage further, with long windows that were designed that way from the outset, and would encourage a crisp and contemporary double-deck look that would become widespread in the 1970s.

The next stage in bus design would be played out against massive changes to the bus industry. In 1969 the two major bus groups, Tilling and BET, were brought together under the new National Bus Company. That same year the first of the new Passenger Transport Authorities were set up, operating through Passenger Transport Executives (PTEs). Twenty proud municipal bus undertakings were subsumed into the four new PTEs, centred in Birmingham (West Midlands PTE), Liverpool (Merseyside PTE), Manchester (Selnec PTE), and Newcastle (Tyneside PTE), and this would have a major effect on bus design. Added in to mix was another government initiative, the New Bus Grants scheme that was designed to speed the introduction of

new buses suitable for driver-only operation. With a 50 per cent refund on the cost of new buses meeting these requirements on offer, operators would take full advantage of this unexpected windfall, which in turn would create supply problems during the industrial unrest of the early 1970s.

Another significant factor affecting bus design was the consolidation of a large part of the British bus manufacturing industry. Leyland had merged with AEC in 1962 and during the 1960s engineered a share exchange with Bristol and ECW, which brought the products of these factories back on to the open market from 1965; and in 1968 Leyland acquired British Motor Holdings, which controlled Daimler and Guy, and the combined Leyland and

Liverpool Corporation had definite ideas about bus bodywork and in the 1950s had received deliveries of double-deckers to its own specification and its first production rear-engined double-deckers were Leyland Atlanteans with this attractive style of Metro-Cammell bodywork. The fairly plain front end was helped by a subtly peaked effect and some of the side windows had sloping pillars, taking away from the a potentially bland appearance. The decorative skirt moulding was another new feature, and the Liverpool design inspired several other municipal fleets to specify body styles that became associated with them. This is a 1962 77-seater; between 1962 and 1967 Liverpool bought 380 broadly similar buses

In 1958 Glasgow Corporation took one of the very first Leyland Atlanteans, fitted with an Alexander body, but when it ordered further examples these appeared in 1962 with an attractive Alexander body that made use of fibreglass technology and took advantage of changes in legislation that no longer required an opening driver's windscreen. Recognising that there was most scope for improving the front end while retaining the basic body structure, new curved-glass screens gave the body a distinctive look. The body was soon adopted as Alexander's standard design and this is the first of many similar 78-seat Leyland Atlanteans supplied to Newcastle Corporation. The large double-curvature main screen gets away from the essentially flat fronts of earlier designs and this is echoed by the upper deck front screen, which interestingly was the same unit used for the rear screen on the Alexander Y type single-deck body. The shapely lower panels add to a generally satisfactory appearance.

BMH businesses became the British Leyland Motor Corporation (BLMC). In terms of bus product, BLMC consisted of chassis-builders AEC, Albion, Bristol, Daimler Guy and Leyland, and bodybuilders ECW, Park Royal and Roe – in other words, a substantial chunk of the British bus-building business. With a range of competing products on offer from the firms it acquired, it was clear that Leyland would take the view that some would have to go, but few would have guessed just how much things were set to change.

Before the 1960s ended the box dimensions of British buses had been relaxed again. Although maximum width remained the same, a length of 12m (39ft 4in) was legalised in 1967; for a number of years it would mainly be coaches that would be built to the full 12m length, but many single-deck buses would be built that would take advantage of the relaxation with lengths between 11m and 12m.

The availability of longer buses persuaded many operators to look seriously at single-deckers as an alternative to double-deckers. There were several reasons for this. Passenger numbers had been dropping steadily across the UK since the peak postwar years around 1950 as private motoring became more affordable and the spread of television changed people's social habits. Until 1966 driver-only operation was not permitted on double-deckers. And a cheaper, more flexible 53-seat single-decker was an attractive alternative to lowbridge or lowheight double-deckers.

The new breed of rear-engined single-deckers prompted bodybuilders to produce new versions of their existing designs, though the move away from underfloor-engined chassis meant that these could be lower built, and this tended to emphasise the length of these buses.

London Transport was probably the most surprising convert to single-deck buses. From the early days of London General, Central London had been served almost entirely by double-deck buses. It had pioneered vehicle standardisation on a massive scale, moving in the 1930s from the STL to the RT family, and in the 1950s/1960s to the Routemaster. The Routemaster went into production just as the first Leyland Atlanteans were entering service and it would remain in production until 1968 in lengthened 30ft form.

Driver-only Routemasters were clearly out of the question and so London Transport looked at the alternatives. It half-heartedly bought batches of Atlanteans and Fleetlines and then surprised the bus industry by investing in huge fleets of rear-engined single-deckers. Where double-deckers had ruled supreme, single-deckers started to appear, even in central London. The models it chose, AEC Merlins and Swifts, proved to be unreliable and enjoyed only short lives in service, but it designed its own bodywork, a competent but rather bland style, that was built by Marshall, Metro-Cammell and Park Royal.

Above left: MCW rather cheekily 'borrowed' the Alexander Glasgow-style front end and grafted it on to its fairly uninspiring standard double-deck body. The effect was similar, though slightly more upright, as seen on this Leyland Atlantean for Bournemouth Corporation, built by Weymann. The 74-seater weighed 8.7 tons and includes a feature that several operators specified, a faired-in rear end that disguised the rear engine bonnet 'bustle'.

Left: Northern Counties stuck to traditional designs for most customers, and managed to achieve a satisfactory result without curved glass and fibreglass peaks. This entirely conventional Daimler Fleetline for Trent in 1963 shows that the Northern Counties designers had an innate sense of proportion. Even with a bland front lower panel, there is something 'right' about this bus, helped by the slightly recessed window pans and the faired-in rear end. Compare this with the Roe-bodied Atlantean for Trent on page 62.

Left: There was still a demand for lowheight double-deckers, which initially Daimler satisfied with its Fleetline rather more successfully than Leyland's original semi-lowbridge Atlantean. Later Atlanteans were offered with a drop-centre rear axle to provide a flat lower saloon floor and normal seating on both decks and this 74-seat 1965 East Midland Atlantean has Alexander's D type body, similar at the front to the Glasgow normal height style but with a much deeper roofline and shallower side windows.

Above: Willowbrook developed its own distinctive designs for rear-engined double-deckers, with slightly angled flat driver's windscreens and a hint of the trademark Willowbrook thick front window pillars on the top deck. The lower front panelling showed what could be done with fibreglass and the only slightly odd feature is the ribbing on the front dome. This was one of a famously controversial batch of Leyland Atlanteans for Coventry Corporation – Coventry was, of course, Daimler's home city and buying from Leyland caused a political storm; the undertaking went on to buy Fleetlines, though. This was a 76-seater new in 1964.

Right: Sunderland Corporation was another municipal operator looking for buses that had a bit more style, and worked with Roe to produce this design on Daimler Fleetline. This demonstrates well how bodybuilders could stick to their basic body framing and shape and change the appearance by tweaking the front and back ends. By adding peaks to the front and rear domes, the appearance is changed considerably and the low-set front destination display and the livery application help. The nearside destination display towards the rear looks like something intended for a rear entrance bus and the squared-off rear wheelarch is an odd touch. This was a 1962 70-seater.

Another, arguably crisper, variation on the Roe standard body was this 1965 delivery to Oldham Corporation with flat vee front screens on both decks, and a rather subtler front peak. Again, the livery application differs from the municipal norm with greater areas of the light relief colour, in this case white against the Oldham crimson. It was a Leyland Atlantean 77-seater.

Below left: This ground-breaking design came from East Lancs in 1963, at the instigation of Bolton Corporation's general manager, Ralph Bennett, who would go on to greater things at Manchester, Selnec PTE and London Transport. Bennett believed that buses should attract passengers by their appearance and this design, based on the standard East Lancs structure, brings together various contemporary features – a peaked front dome, faired-in rear end, a brighter livery and subtly sloping window pillars. Other features are the squared-off wheelarches and the translucent fibreglass panels in the roof that made the upper deck much brighter. It was a 78-seat Leyland Atlantean, unusually sporting a Leyland-Albion badge on the front lower panel.

Below: Nottingham City Transport had very clear ideas about double-deck design and over a number of years had bodies constructed to its own design and specification by a number of leading builders. This 1966 Daimler Fleetline has a 76-seat Metro-Cammell body with front curved-glass screens, a distinctive front lower panel, the destination indicator set on an inward-sloping panel above the driver, and a deeper than normal 'notch' above the engine compartment. The interior layout of Nottingham buses was often unconventional, to maximise seating capacity.

Above: Another variation on a similar theme, this time from Roe's associate company, Park Royal. The standard Park Royal body has been improved with the frontal treatment, again with vee screens but with a more restrained dome treatment. The lower front panel moulding is the same as the Oldham bus. This was a 1964 Daimler Fleetline 77-seater for Sheffield Corporation and weighed 8.85tons.

One of the most striking designs of the late 1960s was the Mancunian, designed by Manchester City Transport as a driver-only bus to take advantage of recent changes in legislation that permitted driver-only double-deckers. The resulting body design represented a fundamental rethink of double-deck design, returning to the square-box look, but with a remarkably deep single-curvature driver's windscreen and longer side windows. The translucent roof panels and the livery application were other distinctive features. This was the 1968 Leyland Atlantean prototype with Park Royal body, and this design would be produced by a number of bodybuilders over the next four years on Atlantean and Fleetline chassis for Manchester and for its successor, Selnec PTE. This bus was 9.6m long, with seats for 73 passengers, but later versions would be 10m long with seats for up to 79 passengers.

Left: Although the Mancunian design was an important milestone, the body style was not chosen by any other UK customer. A design that was probably more important in setting the path for future bodies was this 1969 Park Royal design, here on Daimler Fleetline for East Kent. Northern Counties and Park Royal had both been working on new designs that involved equal-depth side windows on both decks, and a move away from the 'five-and-a-half-bay' layout that had become the convention on rear-engined double-deckers, with five full bays behind the entrance plus a smaller bay that matched the emergency door on the offside, just ahead of the engine compartment. On the new design a four-bay layout was adopted for the nearside, with a shorter bay and the emergency exit matching the fourth full nearside bay at the rear. The effect was undoubtedly cleaner and crisper, and one subsequent change on subsequent designs was the length of the rear side windows on the upper deck. In place of the long window seen on the East Kent bus there were two windows – one matching its lower deck equivalent, plus a smaller window behind that. This resulted in a more balanced body. The East Kent bus has vee front screens but later versions would have curved screens and different front lower panels. It weighed 8.8tons.

Left: While other major cities like Glasgow, Liverpool and Manchester were developing their own distinctive double-deck body styles, Birmingham City Transport stuck with this fairly conventional style based on the standard Metro-Cammell design for early examples of its large fleet of Daimler Fleetlines. The result was competent if unexciting, with vee driver's screens and a slightly shaped lower panel as the only obvious concessions to current thinking. This was a 1965 76-seater.

Right: Edinburgh Corporation pioneered the use of panoramic windows on its Alexander-bodied Leyland Atlanteans, where intermediate window pillars were omitted and extra-long windows fitted. Most were 30ft long, but this was an early 33ft version, and although the Alexander J type body is clearly derived from the 1962 Glasgow Corporation style, the long windows and the extra length give a definite impression of sleekness. This was an 82-seater, new in 1967, and weighed 9.05tons.

Right: There was still a demand for more conventional front-engined chassis, sometimes from customers that had tried rear-engined designs and had been less than impressed. Bristol and ECW persevered with the flat-floor versions of the ground-breaking Lodekka, and a 30ft-long FLF version, first introduced in 1959, would become the most popular choice with Tilling Group fleets; it was also popular with SBG fleets that could – and did – buy rear-engined models, and this is a 1965 delivery to Eastern Scottish. Still very obviously a Lodekka and an ECW product, the FLF was more upright than its shorter predecessors, with the same rugged looks. The louvres on either side of the destination display are for Cave-Brown-Cave heating. Note the cream window rubbers, a brief fashion, and the revised and more three-dimensional Bristol grille. This was a 70-seater and there would be batches of longer FLFs, 31ft long, with seats for up to 78 passengers, in effect matching the best capacities on Atlanteans and Fleetlines.

Left: Bristol's late entrant in the rear-engined double-deck stakes was the VR, and initially it chose not to follow Daimler's and Leyland's example by placing the engine transversely across the rear, but fitted it longitudinally at the rear offside. The two prototype VRs were 80-seaters and carried ECW bodies. The extra length – they were 33ft long – and the lowheight build gave the buses a sleek appearance, helped on the nearside by the long lower deck window; with the engine virtually inside the saloon there was no need for a 'bustle' to spoil the lines. A neat front lower panel included a simple grille. This prototype was built for Central SMT, but soon passed to join its partner at Bristol Omnibus Company.

Although a forward entrance Routemaster was built for London Transport in 1962 it never operated in normal service in London, but there was interest in the concept from Northern General, which bought 50 in 1964/65. The short extra window bay to achieve the 30ft length can be seen on both decks, and the result is a neat-looking bus. The main external differences from London Transport practice were the single-line destination display and the sliding, rather than quarter-drop, ventilators. Like all production Routemasters, the Northern buses were AEC/Park Royal products and this one is seen at AEC's Southall works in London before delivery to Gateshead. It was a 72-seater weighing 7.7tons, a full ton less than a typical contemporary rear-engined double-decker.

Right: Following the poor reception for its integral Bridgemaster lowheight model, AEC developed a new chassis, the Renown, in 1962, and while it enjoyed relatively greater success, the market was moving away from buses like this and with the legalisation of driver-only double-deckers – and the government's later Bus Grants Scheme – operators were looking for models where passengers boarded beside the driver. The Renown was a lowheight model and although many were bodied by Park Royal, as here, other builders were also chosen. This 1965 74-seat example was for Red Rover, Aylesbury, and weighed 8.15tons.

Below right: Unlike the Bridgemaster, AEC Renowns were chassis and could be bodied by other builders. Nottingham City Transport, famous for its quirky approach to bus design, bought Renowns in 1965 with Weymann 70-seat bodies, an interesting combination of a lowheight bus with full-height bodies; the extra-deep upper deck windows will be noted, giving the bus a slightly top-heavy appearance. It weighed 8.05tons.

Below left: There were operators that continued to favour 27ft long double-deckers but specified forward entrances. This 1963 Devon General AEC Regent V has Metro-Cammell 59-seat Orion-style bodywork – known as the Aurora in this form.

Right: Some of the most attractive forward entrance double-deckers were the Daimler CVG6.30 with Roe 70-seat composite bodies supplied to Leeds City Transport in 1962. These had the later Daimler 'new-look' bonnet with a wider central grille and wing-mounted headlamps. The traditional Roe body shape adapted well to the forward entrance layout.

Right: Some municipal operators stuck with conventional front engine/rear entrance bodies long after most had turned to forward entrances or rear engines. Leicester City Transport had bought Leyland Atlanteans in 1962 but in 1968 bought Leyland Titan PD3s with Metro-Cammell bodies like this one. The body is the Orion, little different to the Potteries example delivered 12 years earlier and shown on page 49. This style of Leyland front end was introduced in 1960 and replaced the Midland Red style offered before. This so-called St Helens front was in fibreglass and had a family resemblance to Leyland truck fronts; the sculpted bonnet side gave drivers better nearside vision. Leyland continued to offer its exposed radiator until the end of Titan production in 1968. This bus, a 74-seater, weighed 7.95tons.

Below: Approval for buses to be up to 36ft long came in 1961 and the first available models to the new length came from AEC and Leyland with lengthened versions of their Reliance and Leopard chassis. AEC exhibited this 36ft Reliance with Park Royal 54-seat body at the 1962 Commercial Motor Show and this bus, a demonstrator, indicates how design would change during the 1960s with the arrival of longer buses. The overall shape would develop into what became a new BET Group standard, although the earlier examples, like this one, had conventional front and rear ends. The extra-wide entrance was not a feature that was adopted by many operators. It weighed an impressive 6.4tons.

Above: A later development to the BET body was the adoption of curved glass screens at the rear, and in this form the body style was mounted on a range of chassis for a wide range of customers well beyond the BET Group. This is a 1968 Leyland Leopard for Sunderland District with 53-seat Willowbrook body, weighing 7.75tons. The basic lines worked well and it will be noted that this particular example has longer side windows than the Marshall version.

Left: The first improvement to the new BET design was the adoption of a new front end, with a new double-curvature screen, a slight peak above the destination display and, as seen here, the opportunity for operators like City of Oxford to include their established front flashes. This 53-seater weighed 8.5tons and was new in 1962; it is an AEC Reliance with bodywork by Marshall, a firm that had been around the bus industry for some time and would become a significant force over the next two decades.

Left: The most revolutionary of the early 36ft-long single-deckers was this Leyland Leopard with Alexander body built for Edinburgh Corporation in 1961. It was laid out along European lines, with entrance doors at the rear leading to a large platform and a seated conductor, with the front and centre doors acting as exits. There were seats for 35 passengers and standing space for a further 30. As a one-off concept it was unsuccessful, but it was one of the first two Alexander Y type bodies, a design that would stay in production for another two decades. The chrome decorative moulding helps the overall appearance of the bus. It weighed 7.3tons.

Below: Bristol and ECW approached the idea of 36ft buses differently and came up with the RE, a design incorporating a rear-mounted horizontal engine. This allowed a relatively low entrance, as can be seen on this 1966 RELL demonstrator, with the floor level sloping gently towards the rear. The ECW bodywork was attractive, particularly when a more rounded front end was adopted from 1970, incorporating the BET curved screen. The two-door body layout was rare on ECW-bodied REs. The use of a demonstrator followed the Leyland-Bristol share exchange in 1965 that allowed all operators to buy Bristol and ECW products for the first time in 17 years, and many companies turned to the RELL and its shorter RESL brother.

Left: Plaxton built a lengthened version of its Highway body on 36ft AEC Reliance, giving the bus a not unattractive, if rather multi-windowed appearance. It was new in 1962 for OK, Bishop Auckland, which like many independents in the north-east of England favoured Plaxton bodies for both bus and coach work.

Above: AEC's rear-engined offering was the Swift, which shared some common parts with Leyland's Panther. This Swift with Willowbrook 52-seat body was delivered to United Services, Upton, in 1968 and again the body is to BET style. The rows of seats rise towards the rear and the use of the nearside rear window as an emergency exit will be noted. It weighed 7.55tons.

Right: Following Bristol's lead, there was a rush of new rear-engined single-deck chassis in 1964. Leyland introduced the Panther, AEC the Swift and Daimler the Roadliner. This Panther was delivered to West Riding in 1967 with a 51-seat Roe body weighing 7.45tons. The lower-mounted driving position contrasts with the higher line of the windows and the body is the Park Royal-Roe version of the BET design. The gangway rises to the rear to clear the rear-mounted engine, as can be deduced from the rear rows of seats. The front end incorporates an Alexander rather than a BET windscreen, which sits slightly awkwardly, and the front grille is to a style fitted to several Park Royal-Roe products at the time.

Below: Leyland introduced a lighter-weight rear-engined design, the Panther Cub, suitable for 33ft bodies and Manchester Corporation was an early customer. This two-door 43-seater was new in 1964 with an attractive Park Royal body, based on the BET style but with a stepped waistline behind the exit door and an attractive lower front dash panel with a well-shaped grille.

Above: The first Daimler Roadliner bus was this example for Potteries in 1964, with a Marshall 50-seat body to BET style. The Daimler badge relieves the plain front end and in this case the emergency exit is mounted halfway along the body side. The bodywork is low-built and provides an interesting comparison with the United Services Swift.

Above: The Marshall Camair body was a dramatic addition to the range of single-deck bus body styles, built using welded square-section steel-tube construction. This Camair on Leyland Panther chassis was built for Northern General and features extra deep windows that curve into the cantrail – but on the nearside only. The bus was produced in conjunction with industrial designers, who attended to every detail inside and out, and although the Camair did not prove to be a resounding success, it showed what could be done. This was a two-door 48-seater, new in 1968.

Above right: Western Welsh built up a substantial fleet of Leyland Tiger Cubs between 1953 and 1968; this is a 1966 delivery with Park Royal body. The BET-style body looks better on a longer bus, but the effect is modern, with added features like cream window rubbers and a lack of opening ventilators on the windows; fresh air was provided by the two push-up roof vents and forced-air ventilation. This 43-seater weighed 6.25 tons.

Right: The Plaxton Derwent was the company's version of the BET style, with thinner window pillars and a front-end design that owed something to Plaxton's contemporary coaches. This Derwent for The Eden, West Auckland, was new in 1967 and mounted on Bedford VAM chassis. The VAM combined a front-mounted engine and an entrance ahead of the front axle and would achieve success with a growing range of customers looking for lighter-weight buses.

This short-tailed bus was the shorter-length version of Daimler's Fleetline SRG6 chassis. Following problems with the Roadliner, Daimler decided to offer the Fleetline as a single-deck model, allowing operators a greater degree of fleet standardisation. This Fleetline SRG6 with East Lancs body was new in 1967 and the two-door 41-seat body, with BET windscreen and high-set windows, looks clumsier because of the stubby tail. It weighed 8.25tons.

Left: In the mid-1960s Alexander developed the W type body for rear-engined single-deckers, a design that had obvious Alexander features but no allegiance to the BET style body. This 1970 Daimler Fleetline SRG6 40-seater for Potteries has the large-windowed version of the W type body, which was also available in shorter-length versions, with shorter windows and with different front ends. It weighed 8.25tons

Right: Ford re-entered the UK bus market fairly aggressively in the 1960s, competing with Bedford for the growing interest in full-size but lighter-weight buses. This front-engined R192 model has the Willowbrook-built Duple body style that would become familiar in many parts of the country. The attractive front end and the deep side windows produced a very satisfactory vehicle. This was a 45-seat demonstrator for the Glasgow dealer, Millburn Motors, and weighed 5.7tons.

◄RED ARROW◄

London Transport dipped a toe in the rear-engined single-deck market when it bought 15 prototypes among a number of experimental types. It chose beefed-up AEC Swifts, which were dubbed Merlins, and these were fitted with Strachans bodies. These included the first Red Arrows, the buses fitted with passenger-operated turnstiles, a forward standing area and seating for 25 passengers on the raised section above the rear axle and engine. The choice of a smaller bodybuilder like Strachans was an interesting one, but when LT went for production Merlins and Swifts, it turned to its regular suppliers Metro-Cammell and Park Royal, as well as Marshall. The Red Arrow prototypes as seen here were functional-looking two-door buses with shallower windows behind the centre exit doors; this bus weighed 7.95tons. The bodies of these and contemporary Atlanteans and Fleetlines eschewed curved-glass front screens for conventional flat glass.

The spread of standardisation
The 1970s

It was clear from an early stage that the upheaval to the structure of the British bus operating and manufacturing industries at the end of the 1960s would have an impact on vehicle supply and design.

National Bus Company (NBC) inherited over 20,000 buses and coaches. The Tilling contribution was inevitably highly standardised as a result of the policy pursued by the group even before state-ownership and helped by its own in-house chassis and body suppliers, Bristol and ECW.

BET had taken a different, less centralised approach. Although it had preferred suppliers and had developed its own identifiable body designs its constituent fleets were still able to buy the buses they wanted if they could make a convincing economic case. With such a mixed inheritance it was hardly surprising that NBC would pursue a standardisation policy.

It was a similar story for the new PTEs. Between them they had over 6,000 buses, including virtually every make, type and combination of chassis and body. Vehicle standardisation was a major priority encouraged by the New Bus Grants scheme.

Suddenly the manufacturers had some major new customers. Where previously London Transport was the biggest single customer for new buses, Tilling orders were spoken for and BET had to be courted to guarantee custom – suddenly in NBC here was an important potential customer, and then there were the two biggest PTEs, Selnec and West Midlands, with some 4,500 vehicles between them. Up at British Leyland headquarters they must have been gleefully rubbing their hands in anticipation of exploiting their near-monopoly.

Leyland had wasted no time in forming a partnership with NBC, Leyland National Co Ltd, to develop and assemble a new single-deck citybus on a dedicated production line in a purpose-built new factory in the depressed Cumbria town of Workington. When the Leyland National bus was unveiled in 1970 it was seen to be unlike anything that had been built before in Britain. Its looks seemed rugged and unconventional, though they would soon become familiar in most parts of Britain. On top of its unusual styling, literally, was the pod mounted at the rear of the roof that housed the National's heating and ventilating equipment. The modular design, based on window sizes, meant that it could easily be produced in both 10.3m (33ft 9in) and 11.3m (37ft 1in) lengths. Although it never achieved its production targets of 2,000 buses a year, it sold well in Britain, though it took some years to win over pockets of resistance like Scottish Bus Group, who eventually caved in to the promise of quick delivery and, one suspects, tempting prices.

The National was probably not quite the bus that NBC needed. For many interurban routes, Tilling's Bristol RE and BET's Leyland Leopard were probably better suited, but the National quickly became the only game in town and the RE was dropped from the home-market model lists along with the AEC Swift, Daimler Roadliner and Leyland Panther ranges, though fewer tears were shed about some of these. Scottish Bus Group stuck with its favoured Leopard and persuaded Seddon to produce what was intended as a Gardner-engined Leopard equivalent, the Pennine VII.

The National's dominance caused problems for bodybuilders outside Leyland group control like MCW, Marshall and Willowbrook who had relied

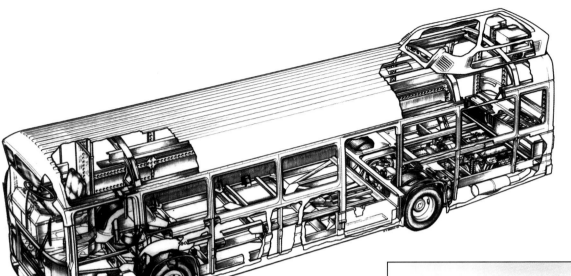

on orders from BET, London Transport and municipal companies. Marshall and Willowbrook eventually diversified into other work, including double-deck bodies, and MCW decided to create its own competition for the National in a collaboration with Scania that produced the Metro-Scania single-deck, which enjoyed limited success.

The demand for double-deckers that followed the introduction of the New Bus Grants scheme was also to Leyland's benefit as the only models left on the market were its Bristol VRT, Daimler Fleetline and Leyland Atlantean chassis. While these gave operators a reasonable choice, there were some who resented Leyland's monopoly and encouraged the development of competing models. MCW moved from the Metro-Scania single-deck to the Metropolitan double-decker, again using a Scania underframe; Volvo, which had been dipping its toe in the UK single-deck

This was the bus that totally changed the UK single-deck bus market in the 1970s, the prototype Leyland National integral citybus. The National was a result of a joint venture by Leyland and the National Bus Company, assembled on production lines at a purpose-built factory at Workington, Cumbria. Leyland, which had a virtual monopoly of UK chassis building at the time, helped its new baby by withdrawing its in-house competing products like the AEC Swift and Leyland Panther, as well as the popular Bristol RE. Although NBC did not have a massive requirement for urban buses, its commitment meant that it bought thousands of Nationals in bus and dual-purpose form. The steel-built National created a totally new look that owed little to previous designs. The bus was available in two lengths, 10.3m and 11.3m, and was designed to use a high proportion of common parts and pressings. The ring-type construction of the body shell and the strong roof structure meant that the National was a remarkably sturdy bus. The distinctive pod on the roof at the rear housed the heating and ventilation equipment and the use of low-profile tyres kept the interior floor heights down. Although the National looked unlike any bus that had been seen before it soon became a common sight on Britain's roads. This is an 11.3m two-door prototype. The cutaway drawing shows the sturdy ring-type construction.

market with its underfloor-engined B58 single-deck chassis, worked with a Scottish dealer, Ailsa Trucks, to develop the front-engined Ailsa double-decker The Metropolitan sold in reasonable quantities, notably to London Transport and Tyne & Wear PTE, but against the odds the Ailsa stayed on the model lists for over a decade and sold to a surprising range of customers, including all of the PTEs.

The PTEs – the original four plus three more, Greater Glasgow, South Yorkshire and West Yorkshire, set up in 1973/74 – were keen to get new double-deckers to replace their motley municipal inheritance and new standard types emerged, though all the PTEs were able to demonstrate that they were prepared to shop elsewhere and most at least indulged in some dual-sourcing. All seven PTEs bought Ailsas, for instance, and several bought Metropolitans.

Double-deckers were not the only crowd-movers, of course. Throughout Europe and in an increasing number of other countries worldwide the articulated bus was seen as the answer to high passenger demand, and the double-decker remained largely a UK preference – although Hong Kong and Singapore were moving to double-deckers in a big way, and there were pockets of double-deck use in places like Berlin and the Middle East.

The first articulated single-deckers in Britain were ordered by South Yorkshire PTE and placed in service in 1979/80. There were five MANs and six Leyland-DABs; the MANs were imported as complete buses but the Leyland-DAB chassis came from the company's factory in Denmark and were completed using a large proportion of Leyland National parts. These pioneering artics had only a short life with SYPTE, but the next batch for the operator, 13 Leyland-DABs bought in 1985, were more successful.

MCW's first response to Leyland's growing monopoly was a joint venture with Swedish builder Scania to import the Scania CR111 citybus with an MCW body built largely to Scania design. This emerged as the Metro-Scania in 1969, and introduced UK operators to a new type of sophisticated bus, but only 133 were built when production stopped in 1973. The high-set windows, heavy mouldings and asymmetric windscreen would reappear on the Metropolitan double-deck. This was the 1969 demonstrator.

business. It did and the new Olympian went on to become one of the most successful double-deck types in recent years.

The look of double-deckers took a step forward in the 1970s. Many of the bodies on the first generation of rear-engined double-deckers were adapted from designs developed for front-engined chassis and as we have seen these often failed to make the most of the opportunities this new layout offered. Then in the late 1960s designs started to appear with four big side windows in the space between the front door and the bulkhead in front of the engine compartment. This altered the balance and gave buses a cleaner look. Bodybuilders that built to this style were Metro-Cammell, Northern Counties, Park Royal, Roe and Willowbrook and the result was some attractive buses, like the Selnec/Greater Manchester standard and the Atlanteans bought for NBC companies.

And on the Metropolitan and Metrobus, MCW did what Leyland had wanted to do back in 1956 – enclose the engine within the body. This quickly became the norm in the 1980s.

Although the New Bus Grants scheme had been phased out by 1984, it had allowed fleets to re-stock and as things turned out this was just as well. Margaret Thatcher's 1979 Conservative government was poised to introduce free enterprise and competition into a bus industry that had been firmly regulated since the early 1930s and where as late as 1985, roundly nine out of every ten local service buses was in public ownership.

Not every operator rushed to buy the National, and Scottish Bus Group only did so when it needed new buses in a hurry – one of the advantages of Leyland's decision to go for such a highly-standardised bus. For most of the 1970s SBG stuck to the mid-engined Leyland Leopard for its heavyweight single-deck requirements and persuaded Seddon to produce what was in effect a Gardner-engined Leopard with the Pennine VII chassis. SBG also turned increasingly to lighter-weight chassis for its rural and other lightly-used services like this 1975 Ford R1014 with 45-seat Alexander Y type body. This shows the short-windowed 10m-long Y type; it weighed 5.7tons.

Although artics were bought for airside use at UK airports, it would be some years before artics made a serious impact in the UK.

Leyland now wanted to apply the Leyland National approach to double-deckers. It had essentially forced operators to buy an integral citybus with an unfamiliar engine by restricting choice and now it thought it might try something similar with double-deckers. This time it didn't work.

With an eye to forthcoming London Transport orders, where LT was looking for something more sophisticated than the off-the-peg (albeit heavily Londonised) buses it had recently bought, Leyland developed what was known initially as the B15 and would soon become the Titan TN15. The trouble with the new Titan was that it was just too sophisticated, was only available in normal height form and was sold as a complete bus with Park Royal-built body. This time operators showed their disapproval by buying non-Leyland products like the Dennis Dominator, introduced as an alternative to the Fleetline, and the Metrobus, an integral vehicle developed by MCW without any Scania involvement. And they bought Atlanteans, Fleetlines and VRTs as long as Leyland kept them on the lists. Leyland wanted to hold on to its customers and while the Atlantean, Fleetline and VRT kept operators happy in the short-term it would need to come up with an acceptable alternative model to the Titan to hold on to that

NBC fleets also bought Duple-bodied Fords for lighter duties. This Eastern National R1014 of 1976 had a 43-seat Dominant Bus body, and weighed 6414kg – equivalent to 6.3tons. The Dominant Bus was built at Blackpool, following Duple's closure of its Hendon, London factory in 1970 and the move of its production to Blackpool; this followed Duple's 1960 acquisition of Burlingham, also based in the Lancashire town. For a number of years Duple's buses had been built at the Willowbrook factory at Loughborough, but in 1971 Willowbrook was sold off and the Dominant Bus marked Duple's return to bus building. The Dominant was Duple's main coach range in the 1970s, and though the bus version shared some body parts, it was a clearly different product, with deep windows, an attractive front end and a generally crisp appearance.

Far left: NBC's continuing need for lighter-weight buses was largely satisfied by the LH model with ECW bodywork, first introduced in 1967 and built in this form until 1979. This was a 1974 delivery to Hants & Dorset, a 43-seater weighing 5.7tons. The rounded front-end and instantly-identifiable ECW look meant that the LH clearly belonged to the same family as contemporary RE and VR models. The bus shown wears NBC's corporate livery, in this case Poppy Red relieved by white, with the fleetname in standard style with the 'double-N' logo.

Left: Following its split away from Duple, Willowbrook continued to offer its familiar body style to customers, but carrying the Willowbrook name and 'W' logo as seen on the front grille of this 1976 Ford R1014 45-seater for NBC's Oxford South Midland fleet.

London Transport continued to buy AEC Swifts into the 1970s, building up a substantial fleet of 10m and 11m versions. This 10m Swift has a 33-seat two-door Park Royal body with seats for 33 and standing space for a further 34 passengers. Similar bodywork was supplied by Marshall and Metro-Cammell, to LT design. The design was more rounded than the Strachans prototypes, with a distinctive barrel-shaped windscreen that would be used on LT deliveries during the 1970s. The overall effect is simple and competent without any of the 'flashier' features favoured by other operators. The Swifts proved less than happy in London services and were withdrawn prematurely.

Left: When this 11.3m-long Leyland National 49-seater was delivered in 1977, Leyland Truck & Bus was claiming that over 5,000 Nationals were in service worldwide. This example was for Fishwick, the Leyland-based independent, on the doorstep of Leyland Motors and a faithful customer for Leyland's mainstream products as well as a few former demonstrators and other oddities; Fishwick buses were often used by Leyland as demonstrators.

Above: The Ford A Series was used as the basis for the Alexander S type, a small bus built in small quantities in the Alexander (Belfast) factory from the mid-1970s. This 1976 delivery was a 27-seater for Grampian Regional Transport, the former Aberdeen Corporation undertaking. The neat front end sits well with the deep side windows and the extra-deep window ahead of the door. The use of rectangular headlamps will also be noted, and these would appear on many bus designs over the coming years. The A Series was not a great success and sales of the S type were limited.

Right: An exciting development launched in 1976 was the Bedford JJL, a stylish rear-engined minibus. The roots of the JJL were in a design exercise by Marshall, the Camuter. Bedford adopted the design and its stylists revamped the looks to produce an exciting-looking small bus. The deep front curved-glass screens enclose the destination display, an interesting innovation that would be picked up by other builders, and the deep side windows gave the interior a very airy feel. Sadly, Bedford dropped the project although Marshall unsuccessfully revived it in the mid-1990s.

Right: The Dennis Dominator was designed as a double-deck chassis to offer a replacement to the Daimler Fleetline, which was nearing the end of its production life. Like the Fleetline the Dominator was chosen by some operators as a single-deck chassis, and this East Lancs-bodied 46-seater was delivered to Barrow Corporation in 1979. East Lancs was more prepared than other builders to produce bespoke bodies for its largely municipal customer base and this low-built body incorporates the grille that appeared on early double-deck Dominators, complete with the very prominent DENNIS name, at a time when manufacturers were giving their names greater prominence on their products. What was a competent body style was rather spoilt by the rear-end treatment, incorporating the Dominator 'boot' and cooling grilles.

Below: Another customer for the single-deck Dennis Dominator was Merthyr Tydfil Borough Council, which took 50-seaters in 1979 with Marshall bodies. The Camair 80 body style has taken on a squarer look with a very shallow roof, deep front screen enclosing the destination display, and high-set side windows. Like other rear-engined single-deckers it has a stepped waistline to take account of the inevitable rise in floor heights towards the rear – the different seat heights will be noted. This bus weighed 9760kg.

Right: There was growing interest in articulated buses in the late 1970s, and South Yorkshire PTE was keen to experiment with the type in Sheffield. Ten buses were ordered, five from MAN in Germany and five from Leyland. DAB, Leyland's Danish associate, built the chassis and the bodies were built at the Leyland National factory at Workington, using a high proportion of standard National parts. This was the 1979 prototype, with 62 seats and space for 60 standees, and its National ancestry is clear though the mid-engined bus was essentially higher than the rear-engined National. Leyland supplied further artics to the UK market, but the main interest in artics really started in the 1990s.

CRM 927T

Left: Leyland's decision to phase out the unpopular 500 series engine produced a revised National, the National 2, with horizontal 680 engine at the rear and a front-mounted radiator, which necessitated a redesigned front end and an increase in length to produce 10.6m and 11.6m long buses. This is an 11.6m version, lacking the roof pod, which had become an option. The LEYLAND name was writ large on the revised front end, and the overall effect retained the National look in a rather more imposing form. The National would continue in production in this form, with other engine options, until 1985.

Right: The attractive Park Royal standard design that was first seen on East Kent Fleetlines in 1969 was adopted by its partner, Roe, as here on a Daimler Fleetline for Doncaster Corporation in 1970. The 74-seater shows the improved appearance resulting from the splitting of the rear side window on the upper deck to give a matching main window and a smaller window. Like many buses around this time it has separate entrance and exit doors for driver-only operation.

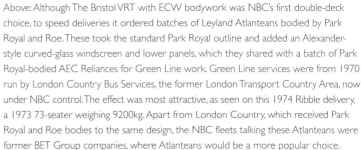

Above: Although The Bristol VRT with ECW bodywork was NBC's first double-deck choice, to speed deliveries it ordered batches of Leyland Atlanteans bodied by Park Royal and Roe. These took the standard Park Royal outline and added an Alexander-style curved-glass windscreen and lower panels, which they shared with a batch of Park Royal-bodied AEC Reliances for Green Line work. Green Line services were from 1970 run by London Country Bus Services, the former London Transport Country Area, now under NBC control. The effect was most attractive, as seen on this 1974 Ribble delivery, a 1973 73-seater weighing 9200kg. Apart from London Country, which received Park Royal and Roe bodies to the same design, the NBC fleets talking these Atlanteans were former BET Group companies, where Atlanteans would be a more popular choice.

Above: Variations on this theme would be produced for major customers. This was the Selnec and later Greater Manchester version, built by Northern Counties and, as here, by Park Royal. The deep front windscreens and the neat detailing of the lower front panels added to the quality look of these buses. This 75-seat Leyland Atlantean weighed 9.23tons. The orange/cream Selnec livery suited the proportions of the body.

Right: The Bristol VRT with transverse rear engine evolved from the longitudinal-engine VRL, which had proved not to be what UK operators were looking for. The first production VRTs appeared in 1968 and when the last were delivered in 1982 nearly 4,500 had been built, over 3,800 with ECW bodies. With Bristol chassis available again on the open market the VRT proved popular with a range of operators, including independents like Mayne, Manchester, which bought three in 1978. The first ECW bodies on VRT chassis had flat driver's screens and a flat lower panel, but from 1972 the BET-type windscreen was adopted with a more shapely lower panel, and this became the most common type of VRT. The Mayne bus is a Series 3 example, with encapsulated engine, and although the body is highly traditional, lacking the peaks and other features of some of its contemporaries from other builders, it has an air of balanced dignity, and manages to look just right. The Mayne bus was a lowheight built to the most common height of 13.66ft; some operators specified 13.41ft high versions where there were particular low bridge problems, and a full-height 14.5ft version was also available, but this was all too obviously simply a higher-built version of the bus shown and the result was ungainly.

London Transport also went for bodies to the increasingly popular standard style for the 2,646 Daimler and Leyland Fleetlines it bought between 1970 and 1978. Bodies were built to this rather square and plain version by Metro-Cammell and Park Royal, and this was the 1,000th of its type and the 1,000th built by Park Royal. The plain all-red livery, relieved only by the yellow front doors, did nothing to make these as attractive as 'provincial' buses carrying similar bodies. The squared-off upper deck roof was a London feature and the barrel-shaped windscreen is similar to the screen specified on the large fleet of AEC Swifts. This 71-seater weighed 9850kg. Like the Swifts before them, the Fleetlines had fairly short lives with London Transport.

Left: West Yorkshire PTE, trading as Metro, followed the preferences of its largest constituent, Leeds, and went to Roe for its double-deck bodies, but opted for 9.5m-long rather than the 10m buses latterly favoured by Leeds. Large fleets of similarly-bodied Atlanteans and Fleetlines were delivered to the PTE between 1974 and 1981. This is a 1974 Fleetline 76-seater, weighing 9576kg. The PTE has opted for deep flat windscreens and a blank panel behind the entrance for the route number.

Right: West Midlands PTE built up a fleet of over 1,000 Fleetlines with this style of bodywork built by Metro-Cammell, as here, Park Royal and East Lancs between 1971 and 1979. Again it follows the contemporary standard body layout, with shallow flat screens under a rather heavy-looking destination box.

Left: Greater Glasgow PTE continued the Glasgow Corporation tradition of buying Alexander-bodied Leyland Atlanteans, though these were now the improved AN68 Atlantean with Alexander's new AL type body. These bodies were rather squarer than the 1962 design and Greater Glasgow opted for the panoramic side windows pioneered in the mid-1960s by Edinburgh Corporation. This was billed as Glasgow's 1,000th Atlantean and was a 76-seater weighing 9012kg. Like many operators, Glasgow had briefly dabbled with two-door double-deckers but reverted to this single door layout.

Below left: Two new double-deck models were launched in 1973 to challenge Leyland's monopoly. The Ailsa was developed by Ailsa Trucks, a Volvo dealer, with encouragement from Scottish Bus Group, which was looking for a front-engined successor to its favoured Bristol Lodekkas. The result was very different, but in its own way proved to be a successful model. Like the Guy Wulfrunian, the engine was mounted to the left of the driver, but the use of a compact engine and clever platform design meant that the front platform was less cramped. The model was soon adopted by Volvo in Sweden. Many Ailsas were bodied by Alexander, producing an all-Scottish bus, and this was a 1979 delivery to Alexander (Fife), a 70-seater weighing 9372kg. The body was similar to the AL type but was dubbed the AV type on Ailsa underframe and normally featured this peaked dome and short-length windows. The beefy Volvo grille gives the bus a purposeful air. Note SBG's continued use of the triangular destination display.

Below right: The Alexander AL type body could be dressed up in different ways – with short or long windows, peaks or domes, flat glass or curved front screens. This 1973 Leyland Atlantean for Sheffield Transport has flat front screens on both decks and peaks front and rear, as well as normal-width side windows. The 74-seat body weighed 9tons. Alexander had stuck with a five-bay layout in preference to the four-bay style that other builders favoured.

The other new 1973 double-deck model was the MCW-Scania Metropolitan, a complete bus based on a Scania chassis. The two companies had co-operated in 1969 to produce the Metro-Scania single-deck bus and decided to tackle the double-deck market in the 1970s. The front end styling with asymmetric windscreens was a feature carried over from the single-deck model, but the body broke new ground and rather tended to indicate the way double-deck design would go. In place of an engine in its 'boot' at the back, the Scania engine was encapsulated at the rear of the lower saloon. This meant that all of the side windows on both decks could stretch back to the rear wall, as they did on the contemporary Volvo Ailsa, and so there was no need for smaller windows to balance the engine area. The heavy brightwork was a Metropolitan feature, and though over 650 Metropolitans were sold between 1973 and 1978, often bought by operators, including London Transport, as a protest against Leyland's monopoly, the type was ultimately less reliable than hoped.

Dennis had been building buses off and on for many years but bounced back into the market in a big way with its Dominator chassis in 1979. This was designed to appeal to customers of Leyland's soon-to-be-withdrawn Fleetline, and it sold fairly well to municipal, PTE, independent and even SBG fleets. East Lancs built the bodywork on this bus, the Dominator prototype, and would go on to body many production chassis. It is to a basic style developed in the 1970s, a pleasantly-proportioned five-bay design, here with a distinctive Dennis grille. East Lancs could supply this body with different front end and screen layouts, rather as Alexander did.

Deregulation and uncertainty
The 1980s and early 1990s

When the Thatcher government deregulated Britain's express coach services in 1980 the bus industry guessed that local bus services would follow. They did in 1986, outside London and Northern Ireland, and just to spice things up a bit the government started selling off the NBC fleets into private hands at the same time. The mood of uncertainty that was created by these actions was exacerbated by the general economic downturn. The mid-1980s were not the happiest years for the bus industry, operating or manufacturing. Bulk orders placed by NBC suddenly dried up and the managers who had mortgaged their homes to raise money to buy their own companies quickly realised that they couldn't afford to fight competition, pay off loans *and* shell out for new buses at the same time. New *large* buses, anyway.

If there is one iconic type that emerged from that period it's the minibus. Before the 1980s most minibuses had been used for specialised work, often in rural areas and for community transport, but the idea that cheap, disposable minibuses could be used in place of double-deckers on urban work was a novel one.

The argument was that minibuses could be bought cheaply, with parts easily and cheaply available from local dealers, and could be driven by lower-paid drivers, often youngsters in their first jobs. In place of a 30-minute frequency provided by a 74-seat Bristol VRT, the argument went, minibuses could provide a frequent service – sometimes up to 12 an hour – that would appeal to passengers and even with 16-seaters would provide more seats per hour.

The 1980s were a time of great uncertainty in the UK bus business with orders for new buses declining sharply against the threat of privatisation of state-owned companies and deregulation of local bus routes. The short-term answer for many operators was small buses, used on high frequencies in place of full-size vehicles. Drivers could be paid less for driving smaller buses and the buses themselves and their maintenance costs were relatively cheap. The Ford Transit was a popular choice at this time, often supplied as panel vans and converted to buses by coachbuilders large and small. Dormobile was active in this work and this 16-seat Transit 190D was supplied to Midland Red North in 1984. This was typical of many early minibuses with the Transit bonnet, a rather square and upright body, with high-set side windows.

One problem was that what was available were often conversions of vehicles built as parcel vans and were not always up to the rigours of 12 hours of stop-start driving in urban streets. Gradually, manufacturers recognised that the bus market was an important one and produced beefed-up chassis more suited to local bus work.

Initially as operators clamoured to get their hands on minibuses any real attention to design was cast to one side. Some early minibuses looked just like hastily converted parcel vans – which of course is what they were – with small, high-set windows and no redeeming design features at all. Enthusiasts dismissed them as 'breadvans' but the big bodybuilders saw them as a means of staying afloat. The demand for full-size single-deck and double-deck buses virtually dried up and bodybuilders faced closure if no orders were forthcoming. Some, notably Alexander, East Lancs, Marshall and Northern Counties, bit the bullet and turned their hand to converting

and building minibus bodies. The results were mixed but generally these had more of a 'real bus' look – and importantly they kept the factories ticking over.

A new entrant to the bus bodybuilding market, Optare, decided that minibuses could actually look stylish and paved the way with the CityPacer in 1986. Optare grew out of Leyland's closure of the Roe factory in Leeds and quickly established itself as a company that thought out of the box as far as vehicle styling was concerned.

MCW also realised that small buses should be attractive and in 1986 introduced the integral Metrorider, a design that would be bought and developed by Optare when MCW ceased bus production in 1989.

Optare also showed the industry that full-size single-deck buses could look sleek and stylish with its Delta body, designed for the DAF SB220 chassis. Introduced in 1988, it competed with Leyland's successor to the National, the rather boxy Lynx, and bodies like Alexander's PS type. Although the main part of the Delta body was upright and boxy to maximise interior space, Optare gave it an attractive streamlined nose and designed an attractive back end, an area that designers often seem to overlook.

Big single-deckers made a comeback at the end of the 1980s as operators regained their confidence, and double-deckers too bounced back, helped by orders from the growing new groups like Stagecoach.

The double-deck choice through much of the 1980s was the Dennis Dominator, Leyland's Lion, Olympian and Titan, the MCW Metrobus, the Scania N series and the Volvo Ailsa and Citybus, with bodywork available from Alexander, East Lancs, Leyland, Marshall and Northern Counties. By the end of the 1980s they were offering body styles that had been around for most of the decade and were ready for a facelift.

Step forward Optare again. In 1991 it unveiled a new double-deck body, the Spectra, on DAF DB250 chassis. This had a much softer front end than the competition, with wrap-round screens and this seemed to set the others scurrying off to their drawing-boards for Alexander and Northern Counties soon introduced new versions of their existing designs also sporting softer, more rounded front ends.

What would turn out to be the last new design for step-entrance double-deckers came from East Lancs which in 1995 introduced the Cityzen body on Scania N113 chassis, with unfashionably sharp front-end styling.

A new bus that was first seen at the 1988 Motor Show was set to provide the step that operators sought between minibuses and full-size

The Mercedes-Benz L608D was used as a basis for some early minibus schemes, although the narrow body restricted seating capacity. This 1985 delivery to Maidstone & District has a standard ribbed-sided van body converted by Rootes. It was a 20-seater and shows the slightly awkward appearance of these buses. Although this model enjoyed only limited success as a bus, Mercedes-Benz went on to dominate the UK minibus market.

The former Carlyle Work of Midland Red, which had a long and distinguished tradition of bus building, turned to minibus bodies at the time when there was a high demand, and in 1987 Carlyle Works was sold off as part of the NBC privatisation. This is a 1987 Freight Rover Sherpa with Series II Carlyle body, demonstrating how even the unpromising shape of a minibus could be made to look fairly attractive. The Carlyle business passed to Marshall in 1992.

A first glimpse of Optare's design flair was provided by the 25-seat CityPacer, a stylish minibus introduced in 1986. Based on Volkswagen LT55 chassis, it enclosed the front-mounted engine inside the body, with a deep, angled front screen giving the bus a distinctive appearance. The squared-off side windows with narrow pillars helped the model to break away from the much-derided 'breadvan' look of other early minibuses.

single-deckers. The Dennis Dart was a rear-engined midibus with a stylish body by Duple, its partner in the Hestair Group. It created a lot of interest and although there were murmurings about what was perceived as a high selling price, the Dart quickly became the bus success story of the 1990s. The Dartline body style was later picked up by Carlyle and Marshall but most designs on Dart were more conventional. Alexander produced the Dash; East Lancs built a midi version of its EL2000; Northern Counties had the Paladin; Reeve Burgess had the Pointer, later marketed as a Plaxton product; UVG had the UrbanStar; and a small family firm in Northern Ireland, Wright, developed the HandyBus.

It soon became clear that the word 'midibus' described anything that fell between a minibus and a full-size single-decker. The Dennis Dart proved to be an adaptable chassis and buses between 8.5m (27ft 10in) and 9.8m (32ft 1in) long were produced. Volvo climbed on to the midibus bandwagon with the B6, which never matched the Dart's success, and Optare developed the Vecta using an MAN 11.180 chassis.

But there were still operators looking for full-size single-deck chassis and there were plenty of manufacturers out there to oblige. The Leyland National had been virtually the only game in town if you wanted a rear-engined single-decker with a fairly low floor. Seddon had some success with the RU as did Dennis with the Falcon, and the Metro-Scania raised its head briefly – but it was the National's decade.

Scottish Bus Group's preference for underfloor-engined chassis has been mentioned, with the Leyland Leopard and Seddon Pennine VII satisfying most of its needs, and there were PTEs, municipalities and independents that bought Leopards. This situation would continue in the 1980s when Volvo introduced its legendary B10M into the UK and Leyland responded with its Tiger.

But even relaunched and with new engine options Leyland recognised the National was ready for replacement. So the Lynx appeared in 1985, just about the worst time to introduce a new full-size rear-engined single-decker, but it sold respectably over the next seven years. Leyland's efforts to corner the market for large single-deckers with complete buses like the Lynx died even before the Lynx did. For many, the strongest feature of the Leyland National was its steel body, and while some operators kept their Nationals going with new engine/gearbox packages, East Lancs identified a market for refurbished Nationals and produced the Greenway.

MCW also saw a gap in the market for a more robust 25-seater and produced the integral front-engine Metrorider. It would be available in longer variants and more than 1,000 were built before MCW's bus-building activities finished in 1989. This was an early example for West Midlands Travel, and shows the solid appearance, perhaps less pretty than an Optare CityPacer, but representing a similar approach. The high driving position can be seen, and the deep windscreen, neat grille and rectangular headlamps.

There was evidence in the early 1990s of a welcome revival of interest in full-size single-deckers, with underfloor-engined chassis like the Leyland Tiger and Volvo B10M and rear-engined types like the DAF SB220, Dennis Lance, Mercedes-Benz O.405, Scania K and N series, and Volvo B10B.

But the low entry offered by these types was not the Holy Grail for every operator. Some, notably Stagecoach and South Yorkshire PTE, built up substantial fleets of underfloor-engined Volvo B10M with Alexander PS type bodies, though the frame height was rather lower than many equivalent mid-engined buses.

Bodybuilders responded with new body designs. Most styles appeared on chassis to both underfloor and rear engine layouts, like the Alexander PS, East Lancs 2000, Northern Counties Paladin, and a range of bodies from Wright; some were purely built on underfloor-engined chassis, like

the Alexander Q, Duple Dominant and 300, and Plaxton Derwent; and others were designed purely for rear-engined chassis, like the Alexander Strider and Alexander Belfast-built Setanta, Optare Sigma and Prisma, and Plaxton Verde.

But this generation of single-deckers was destined to be short-lived. No sooner had they been introduced than easy-access low-floor buses with stepless entrances appeared on the scene. Such animals existed in Continental Europe so the technology existed but these were operating in fleets that were heavily subsidised; in Britain, where subsidy was almost a dirty word and the farebox supplied most of the income it seemed unlikely that operators could afford them.

Things didn't change overnight in the UK and the final generation of step-entrance single-deckers stayed on the model lists until the end of the 1990s, but once the more conservative operators had got over their suspicion of low-floor buses and their concerns about the price premium these initially carried the low-floor revolution had taken over.

Above: Optare bought the rights for MCW designs, revamped the Metrorider model and relaunched as the MetroRider. This 1990 delivery to Newport Transport shows how little the design has changed externally; there are changes to the waistrail, now straight, and the wheelarches, and of course the grille now sports an Optare badge. There were changes under the skin following structural problems with the MCW product, and gasket glazing was adopted in place of MCW's bonded glazing. Optare would go on to build a further 2,000-plus MetroRiders.

Right: Bus operators were looking for larger and sturdier minibuses and Optare introduced the StarRider, based on Mercedes-Benz 811D chassis in 1987. This had the raked enclosed front-end styling introduced with the CityPacer, but had a more purposeful appearance and seats for up to 33 passengers. This was a London Buses 1988 delivery, for its Selkent district, weighing 4423kg.

Built to replace Routemasters for service in central London – though not past Buckingham Palace – the Alexander-bodied Mercedes-Benz 811D minibuses built for London Buses from 1989 represented an important step forward. The 8.4m-long buses had seats for 28 with room for 15 standees and weighed 4183kg. The double-width doors will be noted and the high-set squared-off side windows. The mouldings above the Gold Arrow fleetnames were used to display route details.

Left: The bus that allowed bus operators to move on from van-derived small buses was the Dennis Dart, initially launched in 1988 with a stainless steel Duple Dartline body with bonded glazing; at the time Dennis and Duple were part of the Hestair Group. The body developed for the rear-engined Dart was very striking, with deep side windows and an interestingly-shaped front end that moved from the convex curves of the (slightly asymmetric) front screens to plain concave panels below this. In 1989 the Hestair Group changed hands but quickly sold Duple off to its arch-rival Plaxton. The Dartline body was sold separately, to Carlyle, which is why this Dart demonstrator, built by Duple, also carries Carlyle badging. Carlyle went into liquidation in 1991 and Marshall took over its bodybuilding operation, continuing production of its own revamped version of the body.

Bottom left: The mainstream builders soon developed bodies for the Dart and for Volvo's 1991-introduced competitor, the B6. These are two early B6s, with Plaxton Pointer (left) and Alexander Dash bodies. The Pointer had been developed by Plaxton-owned Reeve Burgess, and was quickly adopted as a Plaxton product, built at Scarborough. The square lines of both models will be noted, with the Pointer presenting a lower-built appearance. The ribbing under the Pointer front windscreen is a distinctive feature, as is the spilt entrance step favoured by some operators at the time. The Dash body was based on the P type framing, and the shape of the front screen, with the bottom edge dipping towards the centre, was a distinguishing feature. The Pointer wears the Mainline livery of South Yorkshire Transport and the Dash the striped livery of Stagecoach, then becoming a major force in Britain and overseas.

Below: The hugely successful Plaxton Pointer body was produced from 1991, initially in step-entrance form, like this 1993 Pointer-bodied 9.8m Dennis Dart 40-seater for Busways, the employee-owned former Tyne & Wear PTE bus operation. The square well-proportioned body would become familiar throughout Britain, normally on Dart chassis. Step entrance Darts were slightly higher-built than their later low-floor brothers, and the change in window levels behind the driver's signalling window shows that this is a step entrance bus.

Wright of Ballymena had been around as coachbuilders for some 50 years but first broke into the British market with minibus and midibus bodies. London Buses was an early customer for both types and this is a 1990 Dennis Dart with Wright Handybus body working for London United. The flat front end with separate windscreens and a recessed driver's screen gives the bus a retro 1950s look, and the 'W' motif on the lower panel would become a recognisable Wright trademark. This is a 9m-long 36-seater.

Right: Optare continued to add to its range with the 10.1m-long Vecta on MAN 11.190 chassis. Like the longer Delta, it used Alusuisse framing methods, but had a rather flatter front end, though it clearly belongs to the same family. This is a 1993 42-seater for Tees & District.

Below: A Northern Counties Paladin body for First's Greater Manchester North, shows the effect of a deep double-curvature screen on what is basically a square body design. This 39-seat 9.8m Paladin 2 on Dennis Dart was new in 1995 and wears the halfway-house livery that predated the FirstGroup corporate 'Barbie' style.

Below: A newcomer to big bus bodybuilding was Wadham Stringer, which launched its Vanguard model in 1979, built at Waterlooville, Hampshire. The Vanguard was mounted on a range of chassis, built to different sizes, and customers included the Ministry of Defence. The Vanguard had a distinctive and not unattractive appearance, with a curved-glass windscreen, a shallow roofline and a suggestion of a pod at the rear. This Dennis Falcon H with 42-seat body was built for Grimsby-Cleethorpes Transport in 1983. The Falcon H was introduced in 1980 as an alternative to Leyland's withdrawn Bristol RE. This bus weighed 9760kg.

Above: Some operators stuck to more conventional solutions. The conservative Central SMT company followed its large fleet of Alexander Y type-bodied Leyland Leopards with Alexander TS type Leyland Tigers. The T type had been introduced as a dual-purpose body and in 1983 it was facelifted to produce the TC and TE coach and express versions. From this evolved the TS type for Central SMT, using the standard shell with bus-type fittings. This 1983 53-seater weighed 8595kg. The Tiger was Leyland's response to the best-selling Volvo B10M mid-engined chassis.

Left: Alexander sought to replace its highly-popular Y type body in the 1980s with this design, the P type, designed as a simply-constructed body with export orders in mind. One of its features was the use of flat glass all round, which, coupled with a shallow roofline and a multi-windowed appearance, resulted in a sharp-edged and rather utilitarian-looking bus. This 53-seat P type on Volvo B10M chassis was delivered to Burnley & Pendle Transport in 1988, and the stark lines are softened by the attractive livery style. The P type would be facelifted as the PS type and would go on to be one of the most successful single-deck designs in the immediate pre-low-floor period.

The last Leyland Nationals were delivered in 1985, after some 7,700-plus examples had been built in around 15 years. Its replacement was a semi-integral bus, the Lynx, also assembled at the Workington factory, and it introduced a very different look. The flat-sided body had deep low-set windows and the front screens used deep flat glass. The skirt panels rising around the squared-off wheelarches were reminiscent of the National, and the overall appearance was crisp and square. The deep cantrail above the windows was a distinctive feature and the Lynx was one of the first single-deck body designs to avoid the need for a step up in the window line to take account of the higher floor level towards the rear. The use of bonded windows, glued into the structure, allowed the three rear side windows to have a black finish on the bottom part, corresponding with the interior window level at that point. This can be seen on three of the 13 Lynxes delivered to Merthyr Tydfil Transport in 1987.

Right: Optare was a new name in British bodybuilding, born out of the closure of Leyland's Roe factory in Leeds in 1984. Optare moved into the Crossgates factory and started building bodies on single-deck and double-deck chassis. From 1988 it produced complete vehicles on dedicated chassis, marketed as complete vehicles. The first was the Delta, on DAF SB220 chassis, a most attractive 11.8m-long package, with a sleek streamlined front end and generally attractive looks. The sides are relatively straightforward, but that striking front end helped to make it a popular choice. This Optare demonstrator shows how impressive the design was in an era of otherwise square styling.

Below: The Leyland Lynx continued in production until 1991, by which time it was the Lynx II with a more bulbous front end to incorporate an intercooler if a Volvo engine was specified. In 1988 Leyland had sold out to Volvo and the Lynx continued in production until 1991. This is a Cardiff Bus example new in 1991, a 49-seater. Like the National, the extra bulk at the front end seems to give the bus character.

Plaxton and Alexander products lined up again, this time at the Dennis factory at Guildford in 1991, for these are the prototype Lance chassis. Essentially a larger Dart, the 11.5m-long Lance offered operators a full-size lightweight single-decker. The bus on the left has Plaxton Verde bodywork, structurally similar to the Pointer body but distinctively different with its barrel-shaped windscreen. The Alexander PS type body on the right is more conventional, but represents an improvement on the rather basic P type, with a new rounded front end. Although more PS types were built on Lance chassis, the PS would become most recognised as a Stagecoach standard model on Volvo B10M.

Left: The Alexander PS type body was a 1988 development of the rather basic P type and would remain in production until 1998. The same structure was retained but with a greatly improved front-end structure with a curved windscreen and the destination display incorporated into the screen design. Typically mounted on Volvo B10M chassis, this combination was popular with a number of fleets, notably Stagecoach and Mainline, in 11m-long form. This is a 1994 48-seater for the Stagecoach East Midlands fleet; Stagecoach built up a fleet of some 600 B10M/PS types.

Below left: Before the low-floor revolution struck in the mid-1990s chassis and body builders persevered with rear-engined chassis that were low-built but still had step entrances. One of these was the Dennis Lance, here with Northern Counties Paladin bodywork. The barrel-windscreen Paladin – also available with double-curvature screen – could be specified with gasket-glazing, as shown, or square-edged windows. This is a Dennis Lance for Metroline, a 1993 two-door 37-seater. The deep windscreen and the deep front corner glazing emphasises the bulk of the driver's binnacle. As with many bodies of this period, the impact is in the design of the front end; everything else is fairly bland.

Below: The East Lancs Greenway was an interesting project designed to lengthen the life of Leyland Nationals with a thorough rebuild that produced a different-looking bus with bodywork that was theoretically easier and cheaper to maintain. Some 176 Greenway conversions took place between 1991 and 1995 and this is a 1993 10.6m-long 41-seat Greenway for Blackburn Transport, which operated 16 Greenways. The bus started life on the Isle of Man in 1975 and although the basic National body frame has been retained, it has new aluminium side panelling and fibreglass front and rear ends. The double-curvature National windscreen has been replaced by single-curvature glass and the gasket-glazed side windows unusually have square top and radiused bottom corners. The resulting bus was not unattractive and Greenways gave good service in various parts of Britain, including London, where they were used on Red Arrow routes.

Below: A significant bus for Grampian Transport was this 18m-long articulated Mercedes-Benz O405G with Alexander body, new in 1992. Grampian was a principal component of GRT Holdings, the group that would go on to form a major part of FirstGroup. GRT had innovative ideas about bus design and this artic would be followed by many bought by First, though not with Alexander bodies. The body uses the P type structure wedded to a standard Mercedes-Benz front-end, and features air-conditioning – note the roof-mounted units.

Above: Optare also worked with Mercedes-Benz to produce the Prisma, based on the Mercedes-Benz O405 underframe. It used the standard O405 front end, married to an Optare body, which produces a satisfying result, combining the Germanic elements with the more rounded Optare bodywork. This example, delivered in 1995 to Sargeants of Kington, was a 49-seater.

Left: The first drawings Leyland released of its new double-decker, codename Project B15, showed a very futuristic and strangely proportioned bus. The reality was different, more square and boxy, but an impressive vehicle. This Titan demonstrator shows the extra-deep lower deck windows, to help standing passengers, and the neat lines that would be echoed on later Leyland models. The barrel-shaped windscreen was a concession to London, very much the target customer, and the advanced specification gave London engineers the nearest thing to an in-house design from an outside builder. As it would turn out, all but a few Titans were ordered by London Transport.

Above right: Another model that was produced with London orders very much in its sights was the MCW Metrobus. After a distinguished life as an innovative bodybuilder, MCW's response to the changing bus market was to concentrate on building complete vehicles. This process had started with the Metro-Scania partnership and would continue until the company was sold off in 1988. The last MCW bodies on separate chassis were built in 1979, two years after the first Metrobus appeared. The aluminium-framed Metrobus was a very successful model and picked up some of the design cues from the Metropolitan, with the asymmetric front screens and the general appearance and proportions of the body. This was an example for Reading Transport in 1982, a two-door 75-seater.

Right: The Metrobus got a mid-life make-over in 1982 when a rationalised MkII version appeared. The main external recognition feature was the revised front end, with equal-depth flat glass screens, and the suggestion of a peak on the dome, but the different window glazing provided another clue. The new structure used just three different aluminium extrusions, three different types of fixing brackets and common bodyside and roof panels. This 77-seater for Northern General weighed 10010kg.

Below right: Operators outside London were generally unhappy about the complexity of the Titan and so Leyland produced a new chassis, the Olympian, which quickly won orders from a range of operators and went on to be one of the most successful double-deck models ever, built first by Leyland and then by Volvo, following the Leyland takeover. The prototype, seen here, had a lowheight ECW body that owed something to the Titan design, and became a standard model with NBC companies in the 1980s. The BET screen sits neatly with the balanced overall design, and the lower front panels have echoes of the National and Titan design. There were also normal-height ECW bodies on Olympian, with deeper lower deck windows, and a similar design would also be built by Roe and later by Leyland at Workington. The Park Royal factory had been closed by Leyland in 1980.

Below: Scania returned to the double-deck market in 1980 with its BR112DH model and grew to be an important force in the UK single-deck and double-deck bus markets. This prototype was built in 1980, bodied by East Lancs to a rather square design that was based on its normal structure but featured a barrel-shaped windscreen – perhaps in an effort to appeal to London – and a generally well-proportioned 9.5m-long body.

7The Alexander R type body was introduced in 1980 to suit the new range of chassis available, notably the Dennis Dominator and Leyland Olympian. A major Dominator customer was South Yorkshire PTE, which bought nearly 300 similar buses between 1981 and 1986 as well as some with lookalike bodies by East Lancs and Northern Counties. East Lancs would go on to produce what it called its E type, apparently with Alexander approval, for some years. This, though, is the real thing, with deep windows on both decks, with the upper deck tapering inwards to the roof and the possibility of a range of different front screens. This South Yorkshire Dominator had flat glass vee screens, but early examples had single-curvature screens and later fully curved screens would become popular. There would also be different front lower panel designs, some to suit different chassis, others at the request of major customers. This 1981 78-seater weighed 10412kg.

Below: In an interesting reversal of roles, MCW offered its Metrobus chassis for bodying by other builders. This 1983 example for Leicester City Transport has a lowheight Alexander RL type body, with seats for 78 passengers and weighed 9625kg. The similarity to the South Yorkshire Dominator will be noted, particularly at the front end and the use of the same upper deck front screen. The driver's windscreen is a single-curvature unit with flat side pieces. The side windows are shallower to take account of the reduced height, and Leicester has partly disguised the difference in levels between the upper deck front and side windows with a maroon band. The main customers for Alexander-bodied Metrobuses were Scottish Bus Group companies.

Above: A newcomer to the double-deck body market in the late 1970s was Marshall, which produced this distinctively-styled body on a range of chassis. This was a 1981 Leyland Olympian for Bournemouth Transport, with a 78-seat body. The lower front panel is similar to that supplied on Dennis Dominator chassis, with the top part of the grille blanked off with a panel for the Yellow Buses branding that Bournemouth had adopted; the top deck windows taper quite noticeably towards the roof. A later version offered an attractive deep upper deck screen.

Right: The Northern Counties design for the new breed or rear-engined double-deck chassis continued the quality look associated with the builder, with well-proportioned equal-depth windows on both decks, a squared-off front dome and a grille to suit the front-mounted radiator of models like the Leyland Olympian, here in a 1988 view of new deliveries for Merseybus, fleetname of the post-1986 arms-length Merseyside Transport company. The slightly clumsy lower front panelling was an adaptation of the standard Northern Counties body produced for Greater Manchester, and was later replaced by a neater structure with a wide grille and square headlamps.

Left: Although double-deck body designs were becoming increasingly standardised, some operators still specified their sometimes-quirky designs, notably Nottingham Transport. This was a 1983 Volvo Citybus with 86-seat East Lancs two-door body, a high capacity for a two-door bus of this size. It retains the Nottingham features that had appeared nearly 20 years earlier like the forward-leaning destination display and the upper deck front window style and the slightly aggressive lower front panel – in this case with an extra heavy-duty bumper. The entrance door is single width and an extra seat is squeezed in ahead of the front axle, and it has square-edged windows. Although it could hardly be described as an attractive bus, it was certainly distinctive. It weighed 9378kg. The Volvo Citybus was a bus version of its highly-successful mid-engined B10M single-deck chassis, but the essentially high floor made it less than passenger-friendly and sometimes difficult to tilt-test because of the high centre of gravity. Leyland's answer to the Citybus was the Lion, which sold in much smaller quantities, though Nottingham also took some.

Right: The growing Stagecoach company was a welcome customer for new buses when most operators were delaying placing orders. It bought long (10m) Alexander RL lowheight-bodied Leyland Olympians for its fleets. This 1991 Cumberland 74-seat example shows the BET-style windscreen and the deep upper deck screen with shallower side windows. The extra length is accounted for by the 'half' window on each deck. Stagecoach went on to build up a substantial fleet of long and short Olympians with Alexander and Northern Counties bodies.

Far right: The Optare Spectra was built on DAF DB250 step-entrance chassis from 1991 to 1998, and this is a 1998 Eastbourne Buses 77-seater from the last batch built before Optare developed a low-floor version. The gently rounded front end caused other bodybuilders to rethink their mainstream products, and the bus has the well-balanced lines that came to be associated with Optare bodies.

Left: The standard Northern Counties double-deck body style evolved, retaining its quality look and balanced lines. This East Yorkshire Leyland Olympian has the more attractive front lower panel, with square headlamps and a black full-width grille panel. New in 1993, this bus had seats for 68 passengers.

Right: Northern Counties added the Palatine II to its double-deck range in 1993, with curved front screens, including a deep driver's screen, and deeper upper deck front side windows. This is a 1998 DAF DB250 with 68-seat two-door Palatine II body for Harris Bus, a late step-entrance double-deck delivery.

Alexander's response to the Optare Spectra was a reworked version of its successful R type body. The Royale was clearly based on the R type but had a new front end with single-curvature screens at the front of both decks, and square-edged gasket glazing. Lothian had bought R types for some years before turning to Royale bodies on Volvo Olympian chassis. The facelift was successful and the Royale was built in 9.6m and 10m versions, to lowheight and full height specifications. This was a 1997 two-door 10m full-height bus with seats for 81 passengers. Note the use of black paint on the side window pillars, a popular effect that gave the side elevation and just a hint of the clean lines of bonded glazing. The extra length is accommodated with the 'half-window' on the bodyside.

The low-floor revolution

The years from 1995

Interest in low-floor single-deckers in the UK was initially sparked by Merseytravel, the Merseyside PTE, which brought four buses over to Britain in 1992 to demonstrate what the Continentals had already done. There was a Den Oudsten, an MAN/Berkhof, a Neoplan and a Van Hool, and these gave operators a chance to see this new breed up close. Merseyside went a step further and ordered 13 Neoplans for its Smart services and one of these was the first low-floor single-decker to enter service in Britain, followed by a Scania/East Lancs MaxCi for Tayside. The Neoplan was an all-German product and the MaxCi had a British-built body to Swedish design, so the first real UK-design low-floor buses were delivered to London.

London Buses decided that it should investigate this new approach and ordered 68 low-floor buses, a mix of Dennis Lance SLF and Scania N113 chassis all bodied by Wright. This was a brave move by all parties but helped to give Wright, a family-owned firm based in Ballymena, a firm foothold on the market when the low-floor revolution really took off.

These entered service in 1994 and there was a brief hiatus while other UK builders caught up. Other pioneering low-floor single-deckers for UK operators were Dennis Lance SLF with Dutch-built Berkhof bodies and a Volvo B10L with Swedish-built Säffle body, though the same design would be built under licence by Alexander (Belfast) as the Ultra and would find favour with Citybus in Northern Ireland.

It was left to Dennis to restore national pride. Recognising that the step-entrance Dart succeeded because it was a simple and competitively-priced product, Dennis reinvented the Dart as the Dart SLF (Super Low Floor)

and suddenly low-floor buses were within the reach of every operator that wanted them.

The Dart SLF was conceived with Plaxton's low-floor version of its market-leading Pointer body and soon other bodybuilders were queuing up to body the chassis. Alexander produced the ALX200, Marshall the Capital, Wright the Crusader, but the Pointer continued to outsell them all.

Most low-floor single-deckers for UK operators were strictly low-entry buses with a raised section from the rear axle back, while true low-floor buses have a flat gangway right to the back though usually with plinth-mounted seats. The term 'low-floor' is commonly used to cover both types.

There were still operators who wanted something more substantial than a Dart and DAF (renamed VDL from 2003) offered a low-floor version of the SB220, Scania the L113 and later the L94, and Volvo the B10BLE, B7L and the B7RLE. Dennis and Optare stuck with lighter-weight vehicles. The Dart was produced in ever-longer versions, up to 11.3m (37ft 1in) long, while Optare continued to do its own thing with the Excel and later the Tempo and Versa. Volvo inevitably wanted a slice of the Dart market and came up with the B6LE and later the B6BLE, but neither gave the Dart a proper run for its money.

Bodies for the heavyweight single-deckers came from Alexander, whose ALX300 was a scaled-up version of its ALX200 midibus body; from East Lancs, with its Flyte; the Hungarian builder Ikarus on DAF SB220; Plaxton with its short-lived Prestige; and Wright with what became known as its Classic range, with a sometimes confusing list of model names.

The next generation of designs for low-floor single-deckers came with the Alexander Dennis Enviro200 Dart and Enviro300, East Lancs Myllennium and Esteem, Plaxton Centro and Wright Millennium ranges.

The previously separate and long-standing Alexander and Plaxton bodybuilding businesses, and the Dennis chassis building business, had come together in 2000 as TransBus International, part of the Mayflower Corporation, but when Mayflower collapsed in 2004 it looked as if these cornerstones of the UK bus building industry could disappear. Alexander and Dennis bounced back as Alexander Dennis and acquired Plaxton in 2007 to reassemble TransBus on a firmer foundation.

It was inevitable that low-floor double-deckers would follow the widespread acceptance of low-floor single-deckers and DAF and Volvo were quick to produce chassis for the UK market, unveiling their offerings in 1997. DAF's DB250 was bodied initially by Optare with a low-floor version of its Spectra body, though at first glance this was difficult to distinguish from a step-entrance Spectra. Volvo's bus was based on its B7L chassis, normally available as a single-decker, but UK operators were unhappy with its rear corner-mounted engine and long rear overhang and forced Volvo back to the drawing-board. The body on the Volvo was built by Plaxton – actually Northern Counties at Wigan following its acquisition by Plaxton in 1995 – and offered a thoroughly modern new look that owed little to previous Wigan designs. The President body would go on to become one of the most popular low-floor choices.

Alexander followed with its ALX400, quickly adopted by Stagecoach as its standard model on Dennis Trident chassis, and the Trident benefited from Volvo's misjudgement with the B7L. When it got its act together in 1999 with the new UK-targeted B7TL chassis, the playing-field was effectively levelled.

Scania's low-floor double-deck offering was the N94UD, bodied by East Lancs as the OmniDekka, and later at a Scania factory in Poland as the OmniCity double-deck. A later entrant to the double-deck market was the MAN ND243, in 2006. Alexander Dennis and Volvo updated their ranges in 2005/06 with the Enviro400 and B9TL chassis meeting Euro4 (and sometimes Euro5) emission requirements.

Low-floor bodies on double-deck chassis were quickly into their second generation. Wright, which has made much of the running in the UK bus scene in recent years, produced its first-ever double-deck body in 2001, the Gemini, which combined the windscreen and lower front dash design of the Millennium range with an arched upper deck that mirrored the shape of the lower screen. Alexander Dennis, having survived the trauma of the Mayflower/TransBus collapse, bounced back in 2005 with a new model, the Enviro400, with equally distinctive styling, and East Lancs followed in 2006 with its attractive Olympus.

By the early 1990s there was a move towards low-floor – or at least low-entry – buses of the type entering service in Continental Europe, and the first new-generation low-floor buses to enter service in the UK were Neoplans imported from Germany. The first UK-bodied low-floor buses were ordered by London Buses and were Dennis Lance SLF and Scania N113CRL models with bodywork by Wright of Ballymena. Wright had been around for some 50 years and had built minibuses and Dennis Darts for various operators, including London Buses. These were delivered to London Buses companies that were on the brink of privatisation. This was a 1994 Leaside Scania with Wright Pathfinder body, introducing a look that would become very familiar throughout the UK over the next five years. The attractive proportions combined well with a rounded front end that included a stylised Wright 'W' as part of the lower panelling. Bodies like this would be built on a wide range of chassis, and would carry a sometimes-bewildering range of model names.

The next goal became the low-floor minibus. Marshall produced its Minibus in 1995 but this was not a happy bus, and Optare demonstrated that it had not lost its touch when it introduced the Solo in 1997. This proved to be a popular model, available in a wide range of length and width options and was only really challenged by Plaxton's Primo in 2005. Optare introduced an improved version, the Solo SR, in 2007.

After a couple of false starts in the 1970s and 1980s, articulated buses started to enter service in the UK in serious numbers in the 1990s. The GRT Bus Group, predecessor of First, started the ball rolling with an Alexander-bodied Mercedes-Benz O405G in 1992 and First bought Wright-bodied Volvo low-floor artics for its fleet from 1999 as well as imported Mercedes-Benz Citaros for its London fleet. The Citaro artic was also the choice of other London operators and examples were bought for service in other parts of the UK. Other imported artic types were Mercedes-Benz O405Gs and Scania OmniCitys.

The natural development of low-floor bodies continued, and continues to this day. Alexander's ALX200, ALX300 and ALX400 models – midibus, full-size single-deck and double-deck respectively – were gradually replaced by the Enviro range which again picked up the 200, 300 and 400 model numbers. Like the Alexander range, these demonstrated a family appearance that runs through the range, sharing certain distinctive design features.

East Lancs also went for the family resemblance approach with a range that included the Spryte midibus, Flyte single-decker, and a double-deck range with model names that depended on the chassis they were mounted on – Lolyne on Dennis Trident, Vyking on Volvo B7TL, Lowlander on DAF/VDL and OmniDekka on Scania.

Wright developed an advanced artic single-decker, the StreetCar, based on Volvo B7LA chassis and designed to provide an alternative to light rail. First adopted the design for its 'ftr' networks that started in York and Leeds.

Where once bodybuilders could – and were allowed to – build on virtually any chassis that a customer wanted, in recent years liaisons have been formed between certain chassis and bodybuilders that have led to some combinations becoming very familiar and others rare to the point of being non-existent.

In recent years, for instance, Alexander has rarely built on Scania chassis or Wright on Dennis. Scania's double-deck partner has been East Lancs, which has co-operated to produce the OmniDekka, although Scania also developed its own complete OmniCity double-decker, bodied in Poland.

East Lancs has become the only bodybuilder to build on all of the current range of low-floor double-deck chassis.

In recent years bodybuilders and operators have shown greater interest in the appearance of their buses, both inside and out. Where once there was a point of view that the bus is a functional vehicle and so its looks are irrelevant, operators wanting to lure motorists from their cars recognise that an attractive bus in a modern livery is essential. Now families of buses are offered by the diminishing band of UK bus bodybuilders – the Alexander Dennis Enviro series built at Falkirk and Scarborough, the East Lancs Esteem/Olympus range built by Darwen Group at Blackburn, and the growing Wright range with its distinctive U-shaped windscreen, built at Ballymena.

And at the time of writing these three firms, along with Optare producing complete vehicles at Leeds, and MCV, completing Egyptian-built shells in Cambridgeshire constitute the UK bus-building industry; when this story started, back in 1950, there were nearly ten times as many bodybuilders supplying the UK service bus market.

But it's not about numbers. Rather it's about build and design quality, which is surely as good today as it ever has been.

What became known as the Wright Classic range was available with bonded glazing, as the pioneering London buses, but also with gasket glazing, depending on the chassis, as here on a Dennis Dart demonstrator with Crusader body, a fairly rare combination as Wright has tended to work more closely with Scania and Volvo.

Above: The Dennis Dart SLF/Plaxton Pointer combination offered operators an affordable low-floor single-decker and became the best-selling bus of the 1990s. FirstGroup was an important customer and bought many SLF Pointer Darts, later versions having this revised, neater and more shapely front end with rectangular headlamps. The side windows now align with the windscreen and driver's signalling window, resulting in a cleaner appearance. This 1998 Eastern National example was a 37-seater.

Far left: Stagecoach had a more conservative vehicle policy, sticking to the well-tried Volvo B10M with step-entrance Alexander PS type body until 1998 when it switched to the new Alexander ALX300 body. Here the last PS type, on the right, is posed alongside the first ALX300, on Volvo B10BLE chassis. Later ALX300s for Stagecoach fleets would be on MAN 18.220 chassis. The low build of the ALX body contrasts with the high-built mid-engined B10M, but both were practical and attractive buses. The ALX300 shared a family front-end with the midi-sized ALX200 and the double-deck ALX400, and the rounded front end featured a black apron under the double-curvature windscreen, giving the effect of a deeper screen.

Left: Not all Stagecoach buses wore corporate colours, and this 1997 Dennis Dart with Alexander ALX200 body carries the livery of AA Buses, a local branding in Ayrshire. The pleasantly rounded front-end design will be noted.

Stagecoach favoured the MAN 18.220 with Alexander ALX300 bodywork for its full-size low-floor single-deckers. This is a 2003 delivery, with an 11.98m-long 42-seat body built during the TransBus period. This Stagecoach in Newcastle example shows the fixed glazing and the heavy appearance of the rear end, a consequence of the MAN engine layout.

Right: East Lancs adopted the bolted aluminium Alusuisse construction from 1995 and in 1996 introduced the Spryte body for Dennis Dart chassis. This was one of the first bodies from Blackburn to have a model name that included the letter 'y' and like products from other builders shared a common front-end design with other bodies. This 1997 Dart for Express Travel shows the attractive, if slightly over-bodied, effect, with a body that seemed too wide for the chassis.

Below: Universal Vehicles Group, UVG, acquired the Hampshire-based Wadham Stringer bodybuilding business in 1993 and this UVG UrbanStar 43-seat body was fitted to a Dennis Dart SLF for Mackie, Alloa. The inevitably square lines of a low-floor single-decker are relieved by a few styling touches – the curve under the destination display, the nearside downsweep of the windscreen, and the step in the waistrail. UVG has chosen not to disguise the raised window line towards the rear with darkened glass, and the curve at the bottom edge of the last deep window at least makes it look as if it has been planned. The deep repeater indicators that flank the destination display were another distinctive feature.

Left: The Wadham Stringer coachbuilding business at Waterlooville had been bought by UVG in 1993 and UVG was in turn bought by the Portuguese Salvador Caetano company in 1998. Caetano introduced a new body, the Nimbus, in 1999, with a deep cantrail and square lines, not unlike other competing bodies, and with attractive lower front panels incorporating small halogen high-intensity headlamps. This was a 2001 delivery to First Midland Red for Worcester park-&-ride work, a 10.6m 34-seater on Dennis Dart.

Below: Marshall returned to bus bodybuilding in 1992 with the former Carlyle Dartline body which it relaunched in 1993 in a simpler form. In 1995 a new body appeared, the Capital, built on Dennis Dart SLF chassis. This had a deep curved front screen and its destination display in a dome raised slightly above the normal roofline. The simple lower front panel included Marshall's winged 'M' logo, and the lower edge of the deep gasket-glazed side windows sloped up to the rear. Several London companies bought Capital-bodied Darts, notably First; this is a 2001 10.2m-long two-door 28-seater.

Right: The Optare Versa first appeared in 2006, and was essentially a longer version of the Solo with its entrance ahead of the front axle. The distinctive raised roofline over the front section later appeared on the Solo SR, and the tapered 'nose' is another distinguishing feature. The Versa was initially offered in 10.3m and 11m versions, competing with models like ADL's Enviro200 Dart.

Left: There was still a continuing demand for more conventional minibuses and the most popular combination for local bus use was the Mercedes-Benz O814 Vario with Plaxton Beaver 27-seat bodywork. This 1998 Beaver 2 for Bluebird, Middleton, shows a typical example with a neat body that suits the Mercedes-Benz chassis cowl, and a feeling of quality.

Left: Alexander Dennis updated its best-selling Dennis Dart SLF/Plaxton Pointer midibus in 2006 with the Enviro200 Dart, using the basic Pointer body structure successfully updated to match its Enviro400 double-decker. With an updated Dart chassis this became ADL's standard midibus model. The attractive front end incorporates a barrel-shaped windscreen and grouped small head and side lights. The small window ahead of the front door will be noted on this 2007 London General 29-seat two-door 10.2m-long example.

Right: Alexander clung on to the minibus market for some years, and its last model was the ALX100, an updated version of the Sprint and earlier styles it had built since the mid-1980s. The ALX100 had a shallower roofline than the Plaxton Beaver, with deep high-set side windows and a deep window ahead of the entrance. This was a 1997 Mercedes-Benz O810 Vario for Midland Red North. It was a 27-seater.

Above: Optare recognised that there would be a demand for a smaller low-floor bus and launched the innovative Solo in 1997. This had something of the Excel's barrel-shaped front end and deep side windows, and the designers opted for a rear-engined design to replace the step-entrance MetroRider, but with the entrance behind the front axle, unusual on this layout. This avoided the problem of front wheelarch intrusion inside the bus and released an impressive amount of space for passenger use. The Solo has been built in various lengths between 7.1m and 10.2m, to 2.3m and 2.5m widths, and has proved to be a very popular small bus. This 2000 Trent 9.2m example has seats for 34 passengers.

Right: The Dennis Dart SLF/Plaxton Pointer combination continued to be the UK's best-selling bus into the new century, helped by the range of versions available, including an 11.3m long SPD version and this MPD, Mini Pointer Dart. This was introduced in response to Optare's Solo, which was weaning operators away from van-derived minibuses, and the MPD was an 8.8m bus, typically with 29 seats. It gave operators a vehicle with a big-bus appearance and easy accessibility, and many existing Dart/Pointer customers also took MPDs for lightly-loaded routes. This 29-seat 2000 delivery to Elcock Reisen, Telford, shows the revised front end of the Pointer 2, introduced in 1997, which was cleaner and more rounded than its predecessor.

The Plaxton Primo was launched as a rival to Optare's best-selling Solo, and was sold as a complete bus. Although Plaxton completes the vehicle at Scarborough, it is built in Hungary. The distinctive short-tailed Primo was built in 7.9m length with seats for up to 28 passengers. The result is a neat-looking low-floor minibus, and this example was new in 2007 for Baker, Biddulph.

Left: Wright really broke into the UK market in a big way in the 1990s. The Ballymena-based company had been around for many years, principally serving local markets, but its bodies on minibuses and midibuses impressed UK operators and led to more and more orders for bigger and bigger buses. First Group was an important customer from an early stage and this is a Scania L113CRL with Wright Axcess-ultralow 51-seat body, delivered in 1997 to Crosville in the days before the universal adoption by the group of the 'Barbie' livery. This front-end design would be standard for some time, incorporating the destination display above the windscreen rather than looking like an added-on afterthought. The lines are well-balanced and Wright quickly got a reputation for innovative and attractive design, and well-built bodies.

Below: A nearside view of another FirstGroup purchase, a Volvo B10BLE With Wright Renown 42-seat bodywork for Greater Manchester North. Like the Crosville bus it features bonded glazing, contributing to the structure of the bus, but some Wright bodies were also available with gasket-glazing, a method preferred by many operators because of the ease and speed of window replacement.

Left: Wright continued to make its mark on bus design with the 1999 introduction of its Millennium range of single-deck bodies. The new body was clearly developed from its predecessor, with its deep cantrail, but Wright introduced a completely new look with this deep U-shaped windscreen and shallow lower front panels, still incorporating the familiar 'W' device. A narrow window was introduced ahead of the entrance door and the front end was attractively sloped. This style of body was built on MAN, Scania and Volvo chassis. This is a 2004 Volvo B7RLE with Eclipse Urban 44-seat body for Perryman's, Berwick.

Above: Optare replaced its Excel model with the Tempo in 2004, using the same structure with a more businesslike front end. It was offered in various lengths from 10.6m to 12.6m, seating up to 47 passengers. These are 2007 deliveries to Johnsons, Henley-in-Arden, 12m-long 40-seaters. Optare has picked up the glazed black cantrail feature that was first seen in the UK on the Mercedes-Benz Citaro, and this appeared on Optare's subsequent Versa and Solo SR models.

Above: The Enviro300 was designed during the TransBus period, with a Dennis chassis and Alexander body, and was introduced in 2001 aimed at a market for lighter-weight full-size single-deckers, 12m or 12.5m long, and would later be available in schoolbus form with three-and-two seating for up to 60 passengers. The deep cantrail and side windows sit uncomfortably with the awkward front-end styling, but a later reworking improved its looks. This 12.5m version was supplied to First's Edinburgh operation in 2003.

Right: Alexander Dennis reworked its Enviro300 model in 2007 with the Enviro200 front end, and this produced a better-looking bus, available in 12m and 12.5m lengths.

Below: The East Lancs Esteem body was launched in 2006 for a range of single-deck chassis. The Esteem has a deep cantrail and side windows can be bonded or gasket-glazed. Most have a rounded front-end that resembles the Olympus double-decker, but buses on MAN 18.240 use the manufacturer's standard front-end, as here on a 2007 Stagecoach delivery.

Above: Following the Mayflower collapse, Plaxton was reborn at Scarborough and re-entered the midibus market with the Centro, subsequently built on full-size single-deckers as well. This 2006 Centro for Arriva is on VDL SB120 chassis and shows the unusual front end with small halogen high-intensity headlamps giving the front almost the appearance of the rear end. It has the black panels above the side windows favoured by several builders. Plaxton joined the Alexander Dennis fold in 2007, reuniting companies that had been together in TransBus.

Above: The new Wright body style was also fitted to articulated buses, and FirstGroup continued to champion the use of artics, like this Scania L94UA for First in 2001. The partially enclosed wheelarches will be noted. This 18m-long bus was a 58-seater for First Manchester. In this form the body was known as Solar Fusion.

Left: The Dennis Arrow appeared in 1996, a double-deck version of the Lance chassis, but its launch coincided with the move to low-floor double-deckers and only 73 were built between 1996 and 1998. This 1997 Arrow for Capital Citybus carried an East Lancs Pyoneer 76-seat two-door body, a competent design that shared features with contemporary East Lancs single-deckers like the windscreen and lower panel styling. The upper deck front screen merged into the destination display, a feature that would be carried forward to East Lancs low-floor double-deckers. The overall effect was attractive, with square-edged gasket-glazed side windows and a raised moulding at skirt level.

Below: It was inevitable that low-floor double-deck buses would follow the move to low-floor single-deckers and DAF beat other chassis manufacturers to the draw with the first examples, based on its DB250 chassis and bodied by Optare with its Spectra body. The low-floor Spectra was literally a lower version of its Spectra for step-entrance double-deckers, which could make recognition difficult – the extra-long side windows at the front of the upper deck and the proximity of the lower deck window line to the wheelarches provide the clues. The effect is competent, though lacking in the 'wow' factor that marked out the low-floor double-deckers from other bodybuilders. These 77-seat examples were new in 1998 for R Bullock, Manchester.

Right: Representing the late 1990s move from step-entrance to low-floor double-deckers, two late 1990s deliveries to Stagecoach's East London fleet. The Volvo Olympian on the left has an Alexander RL type two-door 68-seat body, and alongside is an early example of the group's new standard double-decker, the low-floor Dennis Trident with Alexander 73-seat ALX400 body. There is a slight family resemblance but the ALX400 is built much lower with a shapely panel below the single-curvature windscreen and the destination display is contained within a full-width glazed panel, a feature also taken up by other builders. The ALX400 is also a lowheight body, which was favoured by Stagecoach in the interests of standardisation across the fleet.

A Volvo B7TL with what by that time was the TransBus Trident, following the 2000 merger of Mayflower and Henlys that created TransBus International. The low level of the lower deck windows in relation to the wheelarches will be noted; the lower build and stepless entry meant that seats could not be mounted over the wheelarches as on step-entrance buses. The glazing of the side windows is fixed, although most bodybuilders offered a choice of fixed and gasket glazing; some models could only be fitted with fixed glazing as this contributed to the structural strength of the body. Although operators appreciated fixed glazing for the clean lines it produced, replacing windows proved to be a lengthy process and many reverted to gasket glazing for future orders. The B7TL was Volvo's slightly late entry to the low-floor double-deck stakes, following a false start with the B7L model, with its corner-mounted rear engine; the B7TL featured a transversely-mounted engine. This is a 2003 76-seater in 'Barbie' livery.

Left: The main rival to the Alexander ALX400 body was the Plaxton President, built by Northern Counties at Wigan. Plaxton had acquired Northern Counties in 1995. The President was probably the most successful in design terms of the wave of bodies for the new low-floor double-deck chassis. It featured deep windows on both decks and a pleasantly rounded front end with single-curvature screens. The top tapers subtly inward from below the upper deck windows, and in profile the front end slopes back above the driver's screen. Many operators chose to paint the moulding below the driver's screen black, giving an impression of a deeper windscreen, as on this 1999 DAF DB250 for Arriva's London operations. This 10.6m-long bus has gasket glazing, and this offside view shows the slightly messy layout of the lower deck side windows, a result of the rather awkward layout created by the use of a mid-mounted staircase; later London buses would feature stairs over the front offside wheel. The shallower windows over the wheelarches were disguised on Presidents with fixed glazing, resulting in the appearance of a level window line. These early low-floor double-deckers also had inward-facing seats over the rear wheelarch, as can be seen, resulting in an oddly claustrophobic interior. It had seats for 64 – the same as a standard Routemaster.

Right: Like other low-floor double-deck bodies the Plaxton President was built in various lengths, between 9.9m and 11m. This is a 71-seat 2001 10.6m version on Volvo B7TL chassis for Burnley & Pendle's X43 service. The extra length gave the President a sleeker look, helped by the bonded glazing, and the flat lower deck window line gave it a more attractive appearance than the Arriva DAF DB250 seen above. The raised window line over the wheelarches has been successfully disguised by the use of black-etched glazing. The use of large-size route number and destination will be noted.

Right: Around the time low-floor double-deckers came along, East Lancs was paying more attention to design matters and produced some attractive bodies. This 75-seat Lolyne body was delivered on Dennis Trident chassis to Preston Bus in 1999. This body style featured equal-depth side windows with only shallow panelling between them, and the result was impressive. The front-end design picks up cues from the Cityzen and Pyoneer bodies on step-entrance chassis, and the lower front design shares a family resemblance with contemporary East Lancs single-deckers. East Lancs built this general body style on DAF DB250 and Volvo B7TL chassis, giving each variant a different name – Lowlander on DAF/VDL DB250, Vyking on Volvo B7TL, Nordic on Volvo B7L/B9TL, and OmniDekka on Scania N94UD. It was also produced in lowheight form, with shallower upper deck side windows. Alexander and Plaxton also produced their ALX400 and President bodies in both lowheight and, more typically, full-height versions.

Below: From 2001 East Lancs offered the Myllennium front-end styling on its double-deck body range, fitted to all DAF/VDL-based Lowlanders and optional on bodies on other chassis. Below the barrel-shaped driver's windscreen is a plainer front lower dash, and the front upper deck window was deeper, with bevelled top edges. This VDL DB250 with Myllennium Lowlander body was supplied to TM Travel, Staveley, in 2003 with a 10.9m-long 4.2m-high 80-seat body. It weighed 11900kg.

Right: Wright entered the double-deck market for the very first time with its Gemini body in 2001, a design that was as eye-catching as its single-deck Millennium range. The same U-shaped front screen is there, matched by an inverted U upper screen and a very arched upper deck roof. The lower deck windows were slightly higher-set than those of its rivals, but the overall effect was certainly eye-catching and the Gemini went on to win substantial orders from a range of operators including the First and Go-Ahead groups and Lothian Buses. This 2005 Volvo B7TL for First's Glasgow operation shows the impressive, sloping front end and the attractive proportions of the body. This bus has bonded glazing, though gasket glazing was also offered. It is a 10.1m 74-seater.

Left: Alexander Dennis reworked its double-deck model as the Enviro400 in 2005, using a modified Dennis Trident chassis and a body that used much of the structure of the previous ALX400, though with dramatically different styling. The front end features an upper deck front screen that curved into the roof, and a curved driver's screen, with a lower panel design that would be echoed on its single-deck stablemates, the Enviro200 Dart and Enviro300. The curved glass in the front doors will be noted, and the heavily rounded shape of the first upper deck side window and the rounded edge of the lower deck rear window. The Enviro400 has also been built in lowheight form, and on Scania and Volvo chassis.

Right: East Lancs won some new customers with its 2006 Olympus double-deck design, here on a Scania N270UD chassis for Cardiff Bus. The crisply-styled sloping front end allowed the company to compete on more equal terms with Alexander Dennis and Wright and was a far cry from the sometimes boxy designs from Blackburn in the 1970s and 1980s. The attractive livery complements the body styling.

Wright Group developed the impressive StreetCar, unveiled in 2005, an 18.7m-long
articulated bus based on a modified Volvo B7LA chassis. Designed as a cheaper
alternative to light rail, ideally to be used on busways or other priority track, at 3.7m
high the StreetCar is taller than standard single-deckers, and has the first of its two
doors behind the set-forward front axle; the driver sits over the axle in a partitioned
cab. The dramatic styling is accentuated by the extra height and by the nose, which
tapers to provide a shapely front end. The spat over the front wheel will be noted,
though this was not found to be practical, even though it contributed to the tramcar-
like appearance. First was the initial customer for StreetCar, with deliveries for its 'ftr'
routes in York and Leeds.